To: Ingrid,

Glynn Taylor

I Cor. 13:5-8

# Taking Giant Steps In World Missions

By

Elgin & Dorothy Taylor

President/ CEO Emeritus

Christians in Action Missions
International

Bloomington, IN  Milton Keynes, UK

authorHOUSE®

*AuthorHouse™*
*1663 Liberty Drive, Suite 200*
*Bloomington, IN 47403*
*www.authorhouse.com*
*Phone: 1-800-839-8640*

*AuthorHouse™ UK Ltd.*
*500 Avebury Boulevard*
*Central Milton Keynes, MK9 2BE*
*www.authorhouse.co.uk*
*Phone: 08001974150*

*First published by AuthorHouse 9/18/2007*

*ISBN: 978-1-4259-7569-2 (e)*
*ISBN: 978-1-4259-7568-5 (sc)*

*Library of Congress Control Number: 2006910780*

*Printed in the United States of America*
*Bloomington, Indiana*

*This book is printed on acid-free paper.*

# Contents

## *Part One: The Beginning Years*

## *Part Two: Our Giant Step Of Faith—the Japan Years*

# Part Three

# Part Four

# Part Five

# Part Six

*We dedicate this book to our four sons, Elgin Jr., Willis, Michael, and Timothy, who shared many years of it, right beside us.*

# Part One: The Beginning Years`
## Chapter 1

### Early Steps in Texas

The spring and summer of 1938 was brisling with activity and excitement for my eight-year-old sister, Annie Bell. She was happily helping my mother, Melinda, prepare for the arrival of the new baby. The time seemed very long and she could hardly wait, for she was hoping for a little sister, as she already had three brothers, Jessie Lee, eleven; John, six; and Arthur Lee, four. Nevertheless, on 28 September, she was overjoyed to welcome me, another brother into the family. So much so, that I became her newest doll to show to all her friends. Whenever mother had an errand to run, Annie was eagerly waiting to baby sit, and even when I grew older, she continued to call me her baby/brother.

My father, Edward, lost his first wife to an influenza outbreak, at age 34, and spent ten years as a single parent raising my seven older sisters and brothers, before marrying my mother, who was 20 years his junior. Together, they had the five of us. They gave me as much love and attention as any farming family could and helped me to develop a good work ethic by teaching me to carry my portion of the work in the house and fields at an early age. When I was four years of age, Mother made me a small cotton sack and taught me to pick cotton and corn, right along side her in the fields.

Our community of Pelham, Texas, which means, "a fork in the creek," is proud of its heritage, as being one of the first towns in Texas founded by freed slaves in 1866. Mr. Paul Henry, (also known as "Bear" Henry), due to having wrestled with a bear in his youth, was one of the founding fathers. His life touched three centuries, being born in 1790 and died in 1915; he was registered on a ship from Portsmouth, England in 1796, listed as a six year old African slave boy, named Paul, no last names were given until slaves were sold, they then were given the last names of their owner. There are several memorials in the area today, and a State of Texas marker on Highway 31 between Waco and Corsicana, Texas.

My three older half sisters and four half brothers ranged in ages from 30 to 20years my senior. They were always sisters and brothers, never did we call any of them half brother or sister. They would visit us during the summer or major holidays of Easter or Christmas, bringing us gifts from Detroit. Their children were years older than we were, but they loved teasing us and me especially, by calling me, "Uncle Elgin."

Being an Afro-American sharecropper in central Texas during the segregation era, my father worked long hours to produce double the amount of cotton; corn; watermelons; and peas, in order to have a share in the profit. He would also work on other farms some weekends to earn extra cash, since he received no cash in hand from his own farm, only a share of the crops.

My growing up years, were exciting for a small town lad. I participated in many church programs through singing and giving short speeches during special celebrations, at both the Methodist and Baptist churches.

My father was a Pastor's Stewart at the Wesleyan Methodist church, where at age 14, they appointed me the custodian. Pie read short devotions to us most evenings and longer ones on the weekends. My mother had grownup in the Baptist church but moved her membership to the Methodist church upon marrying my father, thus we were welcomed at all the churches, including the African Methodist Church. My mother was a wonderful Christian and given to much prayer, and a sweet example of a godly mother and stepmother, by never treating the first seven any differently than her own, and working hard to maintain family unity.

Some Sundays, I would sing in the choir or men's quartet at my church at 11 am, as we always held shorter services, then go to the Baptist or AME and sing at their service. This trans-denominationalism prepared me for a later non-denominational ministry in missions. My spiritual outlook was broadening, while instilling a great Christian heritage, moral values, Biblical knowledge, and preparation, for the various opportunities that opened for me in worldwide ministry.

Dean Kelly, my best friend and I, were very close, we spent most evenings and weekends together. Many times after a night out, I became the designated driver for my brother, Arthur and my nephew, Edgar Jr. I did not touch drink, after an embarrassing experience at the Texas State Fair at age fifteen. I had purchased a bottle of wine and consumed most of it on the bus. Upon arrival, I was very inebriated and while showing off for my girlfriend, became so sick that I had to duck under our bus to avoid being sick on others. Having been taught to love God and carry myself as an example, I knew that letting drink control my life wasn't what I wanted, so I promised God I would never drink like that ever again, and I kept that vow.

My brother Arthur and I worked long hours on our farm through the week, then worked most weekends driving people into Waco or Dallas for shopping or doctor visits; helped neighbors load their crops; or took cattle or other livestock to the market. This was all a part of growing up in the country in the 1950's.

Even with the extra work, we never seemed to have much cash money. Being a three star athletic, winning the highest awards in basketball, track, and baseball, there was never enough money for sports or school clothes. I personally choose to thresh local wild pecan trees every year, to sell the nuts and purchase school clothes; sports uniforms; and tennis shoes

World War II changed many people's lives across the country, but in Pelham, it changed our whole world! Two older sisters and two older brothers moved to Detroit, Michigan to find work earning a fair wage at the Ford and General Motors plants. Later another sister and her family joined them in Detroit. Three brothers went into the military. Thank God, they returned home safe.

Sad to say, none returned to live in Pelham. It seemed that, suddenly, our large family of twelve and most of the older grandchildren had moved away. Only a handful remained near us, Edgar from the older group; and John, who lived just down the road; Jessie who moved to Fort Worth, and Annie Bell, who moved to Waco. We saw most of them on weekends, special celebrations, and Holidays.

A change was noticed in many of the older people in the community. Their talk moved from Pelham and local news, to their children and grandchildren in Dallas; New York; Chicago; and Detroit; the cities where jobs were open for Afro-Americans.

Everyone began to look forward to and plan for the holidays and the summers when his or her children came to visit. We would sit on our front porches in the evenings and different ones would read letters from their family in distant cities far removed from our small town, yet life in Pelham moved ahead.

In my high school years, sports held much excitement for me and all our community. There were no other activities for the youth. Sports were the cheapest thing we had and we could be proud of the children who excelled in them. Each year, I played basketball in the fall, ran track in the winter, and baseball in the summer.

The youth of the community had great goals; many of them were outstanding in several sports, and hoped to go pro in the future. In track, my goal was always to surpass Joe Curtis Baker, who had the fastest time for the 100-yard dash in our conference. He continually broke the tape at 9.8 and my best seemed to remain at 10.0 flat. At his graduation, I am not ashamed to say how pleased I was to be the "fastest boy in Pelham High School."

In playing basketball, I was a point guard and an excellent shooter. We were the local team to beat, playing all around central Texas. Professor Davenport would squeeze all of us into his old Chevrolet and drive us to games up to 50-60 miles away. We won many trophies at the regional meets, and during state playoffs at Prairie View A& M College. Prairie View was recognized in the 1950s and 60s as one of the best black colleges in the nation.

The trophies are now in the Pelham museum, along with many photographs and other memorabilia of the Pelham High School years.

In all of this, my greatest passion was for baseball, and I could not wait for summer to follow Jackie Robinson, Pee Wee Reese, Gil Hodges, and Willie Mayes on our old battered radio. I longed for the days work to end, so we could be out on that baseball diamond (a dirt field next to the school)) catching fly balls and hitting as many homeruns as possible. Before and after school, we would practice a catch or a throw repeatedly, and batting practice was endless.

This was why so many country boys became highly skilled in sports. We worked hard in our spare moments playing a certain hit or catch repeatedly. When we were not in the fields, we played ball. In those days, it was an old battered or rag ball; two old bats; or big sticks, for the coach would not let us use the good equipment since he did not have funds to purchase more. We learned to catch; run; hit; and slide home in sandlots games.

After four years of excelling in three sports, baseball, basketball, and track, the local scouts for the then Brooklyn Dodges approached me during a track meet at Prairie View A& M College. They offered me a long-term contract to begin with their local farm team, "The Waco Pirates." This was a real dream come true moment, and I was eager to accept. However, in those days, parents and guardians had to agree fully with all contracts.

My parents and I talked it over, but they were reluctant for me to take such a step, not being sure of what would happen in the future. They were not too positive that I could make a good living playing ball all my life. This was just after Jackie Robinson had started with the Brooklyn Dodgers, which gave us hope. They wanted the best for me, but New York seemed so far away in those days.

Being seventeen, I was also eligible for conscription by the military any day, and after much discussion with the family; we all agreed that I should complete my military obligations first, before joining a ball team. It was also felt that I would be more mature and able to hit the ball further with a bit more weight and height. (I was one of those tall lanky fellows, 6ft tall weighing 155 pounds.)

However, the agents gave me a contact number in which to contact them whenever I was ready to take them up on their offer. They said it would be good for the next five years. This became my goal and kept me inspired throughout the next year, I knew that I had an offer on the table and would re-enter the world of baseball in the future.

# Chapter 2

## First Step: "Join the Marines and see the World."

Two months after high school graduation, while visiting in Dallas, July 1956, I spotted a sign, *"Join the Marines, and see the world."* I took my first giant step, by walking in and signing up for the US Marines! We had never discussed which branch of the service we liked, so later I learned, that Dean had also signed up, but for the Army. Thus, the binding tie was broken and we became separated from the time we joined the military. The Marines sent me to Camp Del Mar at Oceanside California. My friend Dean went to another region with the Army. Sometimes I wonder what would have happened if we had both joined the same military unit.

Upon completion of basic training in Oceanside, a White Christian Marine who attended a Friday night outreach rally and basketball game at a local Baptist Church invited me. That evening, after the fun and games, the church showed the Billy Graham film, *Souls in Conflict*, starring Joan Windmill, about the London Harringay Crusade. It brought me under such spiritual conviction, that I gripped my seat to avoid going forward when the altar call was given. I loved God, had joined church, was baptized, prayed often; nonetheless, making a total commitment was made so much clearer.

Upon leaving the church, my Christian friend knew that I was wrestling with one of the most important decisions in my life. He never said a word, just walked silently beside me for half an hour up and down Hill St; He then suggested we go to *The Christian Businessmen's' Servicemen's' Center* over the Paramount Theater, free refreshments.

At the center, we were welcomed by a man from Sweden, Mr. Oscar Olson, who sat with us while we ate cake and drank soft drinks. He proceeded to ask me a few personal questions and reminded me of my Christian up bringing in Texas. Then he opened the Bible and talked about the great sacrifice Jesus had made for my sins. A short time later, someone began singing and the center's leader, Rev. Howard Carey, presented a short message.

# Second Step

## Receiving Christ as my atonement

This time when the invitation to receive Christ into your life was given, I took my second and most important "Giant Step," towards God and his forgiveness in Christ.

Mr. Olson came along side me; opened his Bible; shared more of God's plan of salvation; and led me in the sinner's prayer. This seemed so simple when written here, but I knew that God changed my life forever when I left that meeting. I had been brought up in church, so the message was not entirely new, but somehow it had been presented in a clearer and more Biblical way, requiring immediate action on my part.

Attending weekly Bible studies at the Servicemen's Center, made me hungry for the truth of the Gospel and I attended every activity faithfully. Many beloved Christians came alongside me to encourage me in my newfound faith. They began teaching; guiding; and training me in my Christian walk. Howard took a personal interest in me, later he wrote me letters of encouragement, and occasionally, sent gifts to our ministry. This foundation became my rock upon my arrival in Japan a few weeks after completing basic training in Oceanside.

I was reluctant to ship out to Okinawa, Japan, for it did not have a good reputation as the best place for a new Christian. The people who had been there, bragged about all the debauchery and brothels there, and how they planned to spend their next eighteen months. I decided I must not leave my base and the barracks, but work and attend the chapel often. I feared that I would not have the fortitude to stand against being thrust into such an onslaught of sin.

As a new believer, I had the zeal and desire to become a strong and "true Christian." I had seen so many who talked the talk but did not walk the walk. Therefore, you can probably imagine how alarmed I was on that ship as we headed for "The Keystone" of the Pacific. However, this led me to pray and seek God in a deeper way; I began pleading for God's directions and for a transfer to a different assignment.

However, God did not change the assignment, but began leading me to various scriptures that I had not noticed before, (hence, I know it was HIS leading not my own). The first verse he gave me was: "There has no temptation taken you, but such as is common to man, but God is faithful, who will not suffer you to be tempted above that ye are able; but will with the temptation also make a way for you to escape; that you may be able to bear it." *-I Cor.10:13.*

*This was a great inspiration to me but also contained lots of shock and awe!* I had never experienced God speaking directly to me on a personal issue before, so it really encouraged my heart.

Being uplifted and inspired to pray and seek God more, I now read my Bible twice daily and believed I could trust God to handle my life and all of those so called "fun things" on Okinawa. The first two weeks after landing on the Island, I refused to go off the base at Camp Courtney during free time, for I now knew that it was even worst than I had imagined, brothels; gaming houses; and beer gardens; abounded on every street corner.

After our third week there, a Christian Marine, Staff Sgt. George Thornton, invited me to go with him and three other Marines to "The Mission." This Mission, turned out to be an old temporary tent that housed, "The Light of the Word Mission" of Christians in Action, founded by Bill and Adeline Quisenberry.

We were challenged by Bill's overwhelming zeal for the lost, both the Japanese and the Americans. Bill and Adeline were totally dedicated to the task, but they were struggling financially in raising funds for both the mission and for their six children. However, we never arrived without there being either soup; or spaghetti; or stew, with cake or cookies awaiting us. They always wanted to help the US servicemen feel at home. Of course, by our sensing their greater need, we all recognized the need to bring more food along on our visits, as they could not purchase American foods in the local markets. We also began raising funds to build a church building, and used our free time to assist Bill with the project.

Each week, Bill would remind us, "Uncle Sam assigned you here; feeds you; pays you; but God sent you here! You are to be lights to those who are still in darkness, both the Japanese and your fellow GI's."

Sundays after service, we would team up 2x2 for evangelism outreach. Most of us became life long friends and missionary co-workers. such as Ron Rinnert, CinA Texas Rep; Gary Woods, of California; Frank Eiklor, President of Shalom International; George Thornton Chairman of CinA International Board & Bishop in The United Holy Church;

and many others. We were sent by foot to Futema; then to the notorious "Koza, BC, Street." We never knew what the BC meant in Japanese. However, we labeled it to mean, *before Christ,* to us Christians.

Even through much of America and the military were still segregated during this time, we all traveled together to all areas of the Island, including the area for Afro-American GI's known then as *Koza-Four Corners.* Strangely enough, few missionaries or Christian workers ever seemed to work there, or even visit this area. It was always a mystery to me, as to how they were not afraid of the wild drunken white GI is in one area but said they were deeply afraid of those in another. Sin was sin in all regions regardless of race. The men were not violent as some are today, drugs were not as rampant, but the excuses were the same.

As the work grew, Bill introduced more innovative ideas. The mission was given four or five reel-to-reel tape recorders to use for Japanese outreach. They were dubbed "Mechanical Missionaries" by our group.

The tapes contained a complete Japanese service, opening with a welcome; Classic Hymns in Japanese; a short salvation message; an alter call; closing prayer. Many times, we could skip the mechanical portions of the singing and let our translators lead the singing, using handwritten song sheets. We would also close in prayer ourselves using a member from the audience or a helper to repeat the prayer in Japanese.

Each GI on our team was challenged to select a village to evangelize and plant a church, which we eagerly proceeded to do: Ron Rinnert chose to work in Uezu; Bro. George Thornton opened in Agena; and I begin a church in Henna, near my base, Camp Courtney. Several others moved farther a field around the island.

# Chapter 3

## Third Step: My commitment to Missionary Service

On my first assignment, I went to the village of Henna, and visited the mayor's office. Introduced myself, I stated my purpose for coming. After listening intently for several minutes, He introduced me to the village English teacher, and assigned the teacher to assist me for the remainder of the evening.

We went to the village meeting hall where I proceeded to setup the screen, projector, and tape recorder, for songs and a Christian slide show. In those days, each village had a large speaker on a pole and small speakers in each home for civil defense and other announcements. The teacher made Japanese announcements inviting everyone to come and hear the visiting missionary tonight. A nice group gathered to see what was happening. The tape would play a song, and then a bell would ring for a few words, then two more songs, and a few words. Lastly, a short salvation message was given, all in Japanese. At the close, there was a prayer and a testimony by the Christian worker, with an invitation for those who wanted to receive Jesus to raise their hands.

To my amazement, three teenagers raised their hands and later came forward for personal prayer. I led them in the sinner's prayer, through the translator and they asked Christ into their hearts! I told them I would come back next week to talk with them further.

The teacher, who had translated everything for me, stated he could not return to help me again, because he was a Buddhist. God wonderfully used him that night, and those three young people became the main support of the group over the next eighteen months. The two boys, Chose' and Sayhi' would meet me each week at the bus stop and help me carry and setup the equipment. They were later baptized in the Pacific Ocean, by Bill Quisenberry and me. There was much sadness as I left the island and promised that I would return after training, a pledge I vowed to keep with all my heart.

*(Note: We did not locate the two lads upon our return to Japan; they were away in college. In 1999, I re-visited Okinawa and found they were still carrying on for Christ in local churches.)*

As my return home drew nearer, I was warring in my heart over "my call." Baseball had been my love and I played with the *Third Marine Division* on Okinawa. One night after practice, as I walked across the baseball diamond, God spoke very clearly into my heart, "Elgin, I want you to return here as a missionary".

At first, I debated with God, something I don't recommend, for you will lose. Of course, I had to tell God about my great future! I had plans to return home and be a major league star, didn't He understand! Why, I could support many missionaries with a six-figure salary from a baseball contract. I lost; God convinced me that he wanted my life and service, not money. Papa Bill always said, "He owned the cattle on a thousand hills and all the potatoes and carrots underneath." I fell on my knees right in leftfield my old position, and wept before God and gave my career and future into his hands.

The following Sunday, when the call for dedication to full-time missionary service was given, I went forward to dedicate my life to serve God, wherever he desired. This sounds simple on paper, but it was a hard reality. For a young Black man in the 1950s to be a missionary outside of Africa was almost unthinkable. In most parts of America, we were not allowed to enter a white church, therefore, it was next to impossible to imagine that we would dare Pastor a non- Black congregation overseas.

Many fellow missionaries did not have to think about this issue. They assumed that if you were "called" you obeyed, they had not seen, felt, or known great opposition against their calling, especially if they had attended a church that had a strong mission emphasis. Unfortunately, many oppressive statements and letters continued to come to discourage me, but I personally knew God had called me to be a missionary on the foreign field, not at home!

# Fourth Step:

# Entering Full-Time Missionary Training

In July, after my return home and discharge from the Marines, I was accepted into Christians in Action Missionary Training Center; Long Beach, California, which at that time was called, *Missionary and Soul Winners Fellowship, Directed by Rev. Lee Shelley.*

While home, I was invited to share my testimony with several churches. It was a delight to especially share at my home church in Pelham... Unbeknown to me at the time, my mother, who was suffering from cancer, had prayed to hear me speak at least once before she died, endured much pain to come to that service. It is a great memory as I look back and realize what that evening meant to her. She beamed with joy as I shared my call to fulltime service with the congregation.

Little did I know that this would be her last time to see me? Three months after I entered training, mom died while I was recovering from a bout with chicken pox, and I was not permitted to travel for public health reasons, to her memorial service. Mother's death was a real blow to me, for she had always written and encouraged me as I took steps of obedience and faith to stay true to God's call.

It was a delight to be in California, and sharing a room with a fellow Marine buddy from Okinawa, of German background, Frank Eiklor, now the head of "Shalom International." We became the best of friends, as we trusted God and shared so much together.

Our first assignment was to pray and help locate a building large enough for a residential school. The President and wife, Lee and Lorraine Shelley were working and taping radio broadcasts out of a small place in Huntington Park; using the name *"Missionary and Soul Winner's Fellowship."* This family had been brought home from Italy by the mission board to head the new training program, but had not had time to complete the arrangements for the school.

God led us to a Christian couple who owned an empty two-story house in Compton and they made it available for leasing at an affordable rate. (Later the Shelley's shared many more stories of God's leading and provision as they started the school by faith.) This was an exciting time, as we planned for our future as Missionaries.

Christians in Action was in its formative years and we were the first students, so there were very few rules and regulations, but we became the guinea pigs for the future classes. Our teachers were volunteer professionals, elocution taught by Donna Giles, a Hollywood star of the silent screen; Public speaking by Stan Belland, a lawyer and public relations teacher; and Bible classes by Rev. Shelley, and Norma Dysart, (who later became Norma Eiklor).

You would have been amazed at two fellows coming to you door, one tall blond fellow and the other, tall brown skinned, especially as this was still during the time of segregation in the US. Our main form of training was via door to door witnessing and street outreach. Sometimes people did not receive us well, but mostly, people were curious to hear what we had to say, as this was a rare novelty. It also represented the way Christians should be, working hand in hand without consideration of race or color.

We gave our testimonies and made regular reports on Radio Station KGER; led weekly witnessing teams all around the Los Angeles area; visited and invited many local churches to join us in outreach; at least twice a week we shared our "Spiritual Thought of the Day," on the radio. We also learned how to prepare short to the point messages at a moments notice.

Each Monday, we traveled to north Hollywood to the Hebrew messiatic centre, founded by Rev. Abraham Schneider. He taught us how to pray and witness to "God's chosen people," the Jews. Many of his family members were Holocust survivors and he had suffered much for his faith as both a Jew and a Christian.

We were blessed to meet many missionaries as they returned from the field and made exciting reports of their ministries. Going out by faith and trusting God to provide was an everyday happening among them.

For me, things were just the opposite with a totally different picture. My people could not accept the thought of not having a salary or fully paying job behind you. Many accused me of being out of my head or naïve. Nevertheless, I purposed in my heart that I would obey God and not man, so I pressed on.

# Chapter 4

## Graduation and Deputation

Upon graduation, Frank was appointed to head up the training program at the California Headquarters. I was appointed as a missionary to Japan. This was an awesome and scary experience as I was now on my own; separated from my closest friend, no support base and returning to Japan alone.

The first persons I visited after graduation were Sgt. George Thornton and his wife Pauline. Do you remember my friend from the marines, Sergeant George? He was with us on Okinawa. We had a great time of Fellowship and reminiscing the past. When I prepared to leave, Pauline, asked, "Are you planning to go overseas for four years alone? Don't you think you should pray about getting married first? I am going to pray for you to find a wife who has the same vision and desire to travel as yourself. She continued, "George worked with missionaries over seas while in the Marines, and may people accused me of being a hindrance to him because I don't feel called to travel. When I was a child, we moved from pillar to post and I don't want to move again." You will need a really special young lady."

I shared, that this desire had been in my heart and mind, but my fiancée had announced when I returned home, that she had not desire to go overseas, nor had she plans to be a missionary's wife. Being an idealist, I had thought she would go wherever I went if she really loved me, for we had been exchanging letters for over two years, and she knew what my plans were so the relationship was broken

I knew it would take a miracle for me to find a wife with the same call and desire to serve the Lord overseas, especially out of our Black community. I had only a short period to raise my support during deputation, so I felt finding such a wife now, was out of the question. Again, I was reminded that God was a miracle Worker.

# Fifth Step:

## A Providential Meeting

From Barstow, I hitch hiked to Dallas, as I did not have sufficient funds for the fare, hoping to make contacts with pastors as I traveled. Very few churches invited me to speak. The only church, which opened to me, was my home church in Pelham, and several women's prayer meetings. It was disappointing to note that my church people and other local assemblies had very little knowledge of the foreign field. Many had so many issues during those days, that they saw themselves as a "mission field at home."

One person whom God kept bringing to mind was a lovely Christian young lady whom I had visited in her father's store several years before in Waco, Texas, and had given her information about Christians in Action.

Dorothy Iglehart had been glorious saved and loved the Lord. She accepted Christ at the age of 12 under the ministry of her Uncle Bishop Thaddeus Iglehart; Church of God in Christ Jurisdiction of Texas, Southwest diocese. We had met in 1953 while I was visiting my sister, who lived across the street from her Father's business which he ran for 55 years, "The Eastside Fish Market on Clifton Street in Waco, Texas" *(It no longer exists, as it was demolished after her father passed in 1998.*

Upon returning from Okinawa, I had gone over and told her about my entering Bible school and taking missionary training in California. She shared with me regarding her own call to missions and signed up for our MSWF paper; and joined my list of prayer partners a year before. She had told me that her family was not happy to hear that she wanted to go overseas as a missionary.

I will pause here to explain why her parents were not too eager for her to leave home. Dorothy had graduated from high school with honors, at age 15, (one of the youngest honor grads in Texas). She had many accomplishments of her own, having worked beside her father from the age of ten, as a store manager and bookkeeper. Her two older sisters, Louise and Zeila, had married early and left home. Her Brother, Thaddaeus, was a Lawyer in San Antonio.

By the age of 19, she had also earned an Honors BSc in Mathematics from Paul Quinn College, and taught grades 9-12 at Carver High School of Waco. Her parents were not eager to lose a daughter who had helped them for so long. Similar to my parents, her father was a single parent for six years after a divorce. He married his new wife, 20 years his junior, therefore their children were not old enough to help her father in the business.

Some of the following information will be an eye opener to you. Few Black families in the south had managed to accomplish as much after slavery, as The Iglehart's of Waco, Texas. They were one of the most famous and wealthy Afro-American families in Texas from the 1950s through the 1980s, when many moved to other cities. There were nine brothers and three sisters, all the brothers owned businesses covering five blocks in East Waco and downtown on the square. They also were in various professions such as educators, lawyers, engineers, pastors, and the last one was a State Bishop in the Church of God in Christ, and a Pilot.

Her father was a local DJ on Sunday mornings for Gospel radio, KWTX, A councilman for the Waco District. (Today, he is featured in the Dr. Pepper Museum as the first Afro-American to serve as a Coca Cola sales representative in Texas from 1953.to 1960)

Even though I had no hopes of Dorothy being interested in me personally, I thought it good to renew our friendship. In February 1959, I visited the Fish Market, and was delighted to see that Dorothy was there. She welcomed me and asked about my progress. I updated her regarding my status and explained about missionary deputation (fund raising) and faith promises.

To my amazement, she shared that she was the district secretary for her denomination's youth movement and that she would like me to speak and share my testimony at their monthly rally the following weekend! She would make all the arrangements on my behalf and get the approval of her Uncle, the Bishop.

I immediately accepted the invitation, even though I did not know what it fully entailed. Over the next four days before the youth rally, I visited Dorothy each afternoon .and we had a great time catching up on each other's lives. God gave us a wonderful time of bonding and sharing the same hopes, dreams, and long-range goals. This was refreshing and encouraging for me. It was also the first time since I had committed my life to fulltime service that I had met a young Afro-American woman whose desires and vision were so near my own. Talking to others, they had not understood my call, nor shown an interest in missions.

The Sunday youth rally at Igleharts Chapel, Church of God in Christ (Dorothy's Family church) was a deputizing missionary's dream. Over thirty churches, pastors, and youth groups were represented. At first, I was nervous to be speaking before such a large gathering of Bishops, Pastors, and City Dignitaries. Once again, my training and radio experience fortified me and prepared me for such an audience.

I began with my testimony; presented the challenge of overseas missions' verses home missions; told of my call; and then told of my vision to return to Japan and share God's Love as a missionary. At the close, I gave an altar call for those wanting to go into fulltime missionary service; many came forward, Dorothy being among them.

Today, I often say, that meeting was God ordained and a huge success, for even if few who came forward continue on toward becoming missionaries, I got the Jewel of my life as the results of it; my wonderful wife and best friend, Dorothy Jewell.. The meeting rekindled her zeal and desire to fulfill her own call to missions.

I continued my deputation, traveling to some pre arranged meetings in Oklahoma and Nebraska, also wrote Dorothy often, while on the road. In April, I returned and by this time, we both knew that God was bringing us together, so I wasted no time in asking her to go to Japan with me as my wife. Well, she did not say yes right away, but said she would pray and fast over it and give me her answer soon.

Three days later, she answered, "Yes, I will marry you, and go to Japan with you"! She continued, "God gave me many verses, but the main one was from Psalms 37: 23-25.

*In verse 23, it states, "That the steps of a good man (or woman) are ordered by the Lord, and I believe you are a good man." She continued, "In the 25ᵗʰ verse, David states, "I have been young and now am old; yet have I not seen the righteous forsaken; nor His seed begging for bread.*

"Everyone kept saying, "You will starve and be beggars overseas as missionaries" she went on, "It had me wavering and struggling with my decision. Now I have my own word from God, and I know I can stand and trust him to honor his promises and keep his word!"

What an exciting and happy evening; we walked down to *Ike's Drive-In,* her Uncle Clarence's place, to celebrate, and later I couldn't sleep all night. Now I really needed support and I needed to know the requirements for getting married in Texas.

The next morning, I borrowed my brother-in-laws-car, went to a pawnshop, and sold a few items I had of value in order to purchase a ring. That evening I did the proper thing, and asked Mr. Iglehart for his daughter's hand in marriage. Don't think I got away easy, he asked me how I was going to support his daughter, and if I was really going to Japan? When I affirmed both, he talked a long time with me over being down to earth and the hard work it took to look after a family.

He also stated that Dorothy was an adult and he would not prevent her from making her own decisions. Others in the Iglehart family tried to discourage Dorothy from becoming my wife. They gave her many negatives on all sides, but she was determined that this was what she felt God was leading her to do.

# Chapter 5

## Step Seven: Marriage, the two become one!

On June 18, 1959 with two of Dorothy's first cousins, Jocelyn and Ruby Iglehart as the witnesses, we had a quiet wedding at the home of Rev. Howell Smith, a fellow Pelhamite, who was also well known to Dorothy. His wife baked the wedding cake and arranged the reception. A few weeks later, Bishop T. D. Iglehart held a reception for us at Igleharts Chapel and gave us a linen shower of items we needed to take to Japan.

While planning the wedding, I had rented a place on the second floor of a well-known businessman's home, Mr. Ashford. He had lost his wife several years before and was now renting out the upper story of his house, which was divided into three small apartments.

Dorothy and I rented the smallest apt of the three, but one week after moving in, the teacher in the next apartment left for her three months summer break, and we were given the usage of her kitchen and balcony, at no extra charge. God began blessing and fulfilling promises even with our meager beginning!

When Dorothy's folks came over for a visit, they were impressed by the décor and furnishings, which were very showroom quality and high end. It made our day when they stated that they had not had such nice furniture when they started out. From this encounter with her parents, their attitudes began to change towards yours truly. Her Dad began to warm up to me and we could talk on various subjects without revisiting his former views on being a poor missionary.

In August 1959, after three months deputizing in Texas, we were off to California for Dorothy to attend our Missionary Training College. This is the usual requirement of our mission organization; all persons sent out had to take several courses of cross-cultural training and soul winning.

During the day, Dorothy was in classes, and I took on odd painting and decorating jobs for church members while making contacts with Pastors to speak at various churches. Many doors opened for us. One door in particular was that of Pastor Sam and Gladys Fuqua. They gave us a job painting their Sunday school classrooms. Their church was in Compton, an area that during this time was all white, but the people feared Afro-Americans moving into the area.

Dorothy and I had first lived in a small rear cottage at an elderly church member's home. After six weeks, the she was threatened by several neighbors for allowing us to stay there. Sam and Gladys knowing that we were only staying through December, allowed us to move into a house they were converting into Sunday school rooms at their church.

Two weeks after moving to the house on West Alondra Blvd, Dorothy became violently ill. At the local Doctor's office, we received news that was both exciting and scary at the same time. Doctor Willis V. Dalton, whose mother Dorothy had assisted in child evangelism classes announced that, "You are going to have a baby!"

Yes, I felt excited, but it was also quite scary, for we had been struggling to raise sufficient support for a couple, now it had to be for a family. In addition, I didn't know how this would affect our timeline. We were preparing to leave just after Christmas. Would we have to wait and be sure the baby was fine? On the other hand, what arrangement could we make in Japan? Just ordinary things became "huge."

Again, Christians began questioning our call and quoting scriptures, which they thought, would prevent us from leaving the shores of the U.S. Many felt led to advise us to stay until the child was born then go. Some even went so far as to say, "God wants you to stay here and raise your family before going out there!

Again, God took charge of the situation. We knew God wanted us to go, but we were not sure of the timeline, since so many people questioned Dorothy's health and that of the child.

One afternoon, upon returning home from witnessing house to house Dorothy entered the house bubbling with excitement. "Elgin honey, she said, "I was really struggling with the idea of having our baby in some badly equipped clinic overseas. While mediating and having my personal prayer time, God spoke to me again from my "Life's Promise Verse" Matt. 6:26. *It states, "Behold the fowls of the air, for they sow not and neither do they reap, nor gather into barns; yet your heavenly father feeds them. Are you not better than they?"* She continued, "I thought about all those women overseas who also had babies, God takes care of them, so why can't I trust him to take care of me? Elgin, I am no longer going to entertain people saying we should stay here until after the birth!"

All I could do was hug her and praise God with her over this new victory over fear! I had had some doubts for her sake but now I felt more assured that things were moving according to God's plans, not our own.

We continued to work and plan as we had to complete our support raising; packing; and shipping our things to Japan, and support was coming in very, very slow. We received offerings when we spoke at many churches. Very few made any long-term commitments toward our support on the field. Few Afro-Americans understood what we were requesting. They would say we will send you something, but we could not get a firm commitment. God had already spoken to us regarding continual begging for support. From Matt. 6:33, "He had assured us that He would supply all our needs if we put Him first in our lives and ministry. We plowed on but were receiving little response by the second week of December 1959.

One week before Christmas, and two weeks before we were to leave for Asia, we were the featured speakers on the CinA Missions broadcast on KGER. I gave my testimony and Dorothy shared the new victory God had given her. As the program ended, we were handed a message that Dr. Dalton wanted to see me immediately upon my return home. Thinking that it may be something wrong with Dorothy or the child, I drove Dorothy home then walked around the corner to the Doctor's office at 10pm.

As I entered the office he said, "Tonight as I drove home from Laguna Beach, I turned on the radio and guess who was on? You and Dorothy were sharing about going to Japan with the Gospel. Listening to you really spoke to me, for I was called to the mission field while serving in World War II many years ago but did not obey. God is giving me another opportunity through you." He then opened his desk drawer, handed me a check for $200, and said I want to underwrite your support for this amount for the next four years. My heart just leaped for joy as I realized that we now had the full amount pledged for our support and a few dollars over.

We thank God for our dear brother, who kept his promise for the entire four years. Upon our return home, he transferred his support to a young relative going to Latin America. God wonderfully used Dr Dalton to be a blessing and answer to prayer. We also wanted to thank him in return, by naming our second son, Willis V. Taylor in honor of him.

Praise God also for Rev. and Mrs. James Stakes of greater love Baptist Church on South Broadway in Los Angles. They gave us love gift for our passage and a food box for our Christmas Dinner.

This church remained faithful in sending special Christas offerings down through the year.

# Chapter 6

## Step Eight: Off to the Field, with a pause, for a Hawaiian Honeymoon!

Our wonderful Father loves to pull surprises on his people. Sometimes I think he is looking down from his throne and devising new ways to tease us, just to see like how much like Job, we will react to the test; "for his ways are not our ways."

Our flight on December 28, 1959 on USOA Airlines was fraught with problems from the start. We left Burbank Airport three hours late and minus a few passengers. Upon our arrival in Hawaii, we sat on the plane for twenty minutes before disembarking. As we entered the terminal, officials boarded the plane and stated that USO Airlines was going into receivership and there would be no more flights. *(Those were the days before airlines and travel agents assisted passengers to continue on to their destination. All the passengers were left right where they landed and you had to buy another ticket to continue).*

One young man next to us began to sob uncontrollably and we began trying to comfort him. He was Samoan and had been working for three years to raise the fares to bring his wife and four children to California. He had paid for their tickets on USOA, now he would have to begin all over. We prayed with him that God would help him work something out so that it wouldn't take another three years without his family.

I guess you also get the picture for us. We were assisting someone else, not really thinking that we weren't continuing on to Japan today either. We had arranged a four-hour stop to visit with Grace Brackett and Don and Margaret Messier, our missionaries in Honolulu to give Dorothy a break. Never did we dream that we would be staying much longer.

Don invited us to stay in their home until things were settled and we visited their church and shared in their services. The people began praying for us and sent extra fruit and vegetables to assist us while there. This also blessed Don, Margaret, and their four young children so we were pleased to see God's faithfulness even at unusual times. Everyone treated us royally and took us to all the beautiful tourists' sites; such as, Pearl Harbor; Punch Bowl; Diamond Head; and I was even blessed to fly in a small plane over Mona Luau Volcano on the Big Island, which was erupting big at that time. Hawaii was celebrating just becoming the 50th state! Some of the native Hawaiians said," The fire God, Pele, didn't like their becoming a state so she was venting her anger."

We shared our ministry vision with several churches on the Island of Oahu. One that we shall never forget was a small Church of God in Christ pastored by an Afro-American, Pastor Reed. He was a wonderful encouragement and example to us. Here he was thousands of miles away from home yet he knew this was where God had called him. We know that some will probably say, but he's in one of the most beautiful places in the world so why not? However, loneliness and homesickness for ones family and friends can hit hard even in a beautiful paradise.

God continued to speak from Romans 8:28 and other verses assuring us of his will and purpose for us. Today, we can say we had a wonderful honeymoon in Hawaii; however, we would have enjoyed it more if I were not concern about a pregnant wife who needed to get settled before the baby's arrival. I spent many hours calling back to our headquarters via phone and shortwave radio trying to arrange replacement tickets to Okinawa. By the tenth day, we received good news, the church in Japan had purchased new tickets for us, and they were eagerly awaiting our arrival. The new tickets were on Japan airlines and with much better seats than our former ones. During this time, the propeller planes took 36 hours to cross the pacific, with refueling stops on the Islands of Wake and Guam.

At last, we looked down upon the blue-green lagoons of Okinawa formed by the many continental shelves that makeup the Ryukyu Islands of Southern Japan. At Naha airport, the sights greeted us and sounds of spoken Japanese all around us, then I knew we were back "HOME" again. Bill and Adeline Quisenberry; Ron Rinnert; Carl and Eva Johnson and Shinyu Kunioshi were all there along with several church members to welcome us. I was so thrilled to be back, that I became overwhelmed with the emotions of the moment! The tears and hugs were so genuine among all the brothers and sisters present. They had seen many leave, promising to return, but few ever did. I introduced Dorothy to everyone and now I could show her all the special places and people that meant so much to me.

Things started with a bang, as we arrived on a Saturday evening, and the church was holding some special celebrations along with welcoming us the next day, so they drove us straight to the little Japanese cottage that they had prepared so lovingly for us in Kitanakigusuku-Son. It was a beautiful three-roomed Japanese house, with the usual sliding front doors with tatami mats on the living room floor, a very low black table, a kitchen, bedroom, and an outside toilet. There was no running water in the nationals' homes in those days. A couple who had returned home, donated many of their things to us; a two burner oil stove; a washing machine; a lovely bed and a pump organ.

Even through I was concerned for my wife's health after such a long journey, she was up early the next morning and excited to meet all the people I had been speaking about while away .

They had a welcome planned for us along with a potluck meal. Thus began our five-year journey as the first Afro- American missionaries to Japan and the Orient. .

# Part Two: Our Giant Step Of Faith—the Japan Years
## Chapter 7

### Welcome to Japan

A dream fulfilled! Again, a wave of emotion flowed over us at the service the next morning. Bill warmly greeted and introduced us to the awaiting congregation. We received a tremendous welcome, and all seemed so pleased that I had kept my word and returned as promised, as so many never made it back. I introduced my bride and got roaring laughter from the church when I also added "and little Taylor to be." .I also renewed my acquaintance with several elderly church members; Mr. Asato San and Mrs. Nakazato san, with whom I had learned the old unwritten Okinawan language called "Hogan." This language was taboo, for the Japanese required all students to study Japanese only. Since working with the older church members, I had learned to say several greetings in their language. Blackie the photographer had been hired to record the special celebrations that Sunday, so we were able to join in and be a part of the day.

A new chapter of my life had now taken off and I began plotting my course with the Japanese people, by learning as much of the Japanese language as possible along with studying the scriptures daily. For Dorothy, the first step was to have a safe delivery of the child. On Monday morning, we drove to Naha, the capital city, to the Seventh Day Adventist Mission Hospital. This was a brand new building that had just been completed, might I say without bragging, just in time for us!

The Doctor and nurses welcomed us and gave us a complete tour of the facility along with the maternity ward. We were delighted that it was so nice; clean; and well equipped. God was being faithful each step of the way. I was praying that Dorothy wouldn't be disappointed with the facilities, now we were rewarded with a brand new hospital, along with American Doctors, even through all the nurses, and staff was Japanese.

We desired to impart God's word to the Japanese people, and they opened their hearts to us. Much love flowed toward us as the people began to visit our home; invite us to theirs; and we returned the visits.

One scripture which kept coming to mind was, "(We were) as poor, yet making many rich, as having nothing; yet possessing all things." -II Cor. 6:10.

Being new arrivals and missionaries to boot, to many servicemen and the Japanese, we seemed dirt poor. The US Servicemen were given nice brick houses or large Quonsets with many amenities and commissary privileges, but we lived in a small wooden Japanese house that looked like it would blow away during typhoon season. Yet not once did my wife complain. She even learned to sit cross-legged on the floor at the small black lacquered table, after our baby was born.

As the baby's arrival drew near, our trunk arrived with bedding and baby clothing, which we had shipped from the States, making us feel more prepared for the delivery. Dorothy really enjoyed fixing up the little house. It was unique being half-American and Japanese with its internal rice-paper covered sliding doors; Tatami mat floors in the living and bedrooms; a step down kitchen with cement floor; a built in sink, small oil cooker, and small refrigerator. The missionary couple had left us the refrigerator, which was not common in Japanese homes on the island at that time. The Okinawans cooked fresh vegetables daily and ate the leftovers for breakfast the next morning.

Over the next few weeks, I immersed myself back into the ministry, helping Bill each day at the church office and in the Japanese training school. On Sundays, we would rotate the speaking between Bill Q, Ron Rinnert, and me, with Bro Kunioshi translating, in the bilingual services.

An all-English speaking service was held on Sunday afternoons with special outreach programs in the evenings twice monthly, and during the holidays. We held all Japanese Bible studies for two age groups once each week. The senior adults came during the day and 25 to 50 came early evenings after work.

# Chapter 8

## God blesses us with a Son!

On March 29, 1960, we planned a tent crusade for the Naha area, with a special guest speaker from the US and I was the song leader and Master of ceremony. However, that afternoon during our final preparations, I received an urgent call from Dorothy. It seemed that our child who was a week early, had decided, today was a great day to arrive.

Anxiously, I drove the twelve miles to the hospital praying to make it on time. Upon our arrival, Doctor Tolhurst examined Dorothy and said, "First Babies take a while, so this baby will probably not arrive until tomorrow morning, leave her with us and we shall take care of her. After talking it over with my wife, I decided to attend the crusade and come back in the morning, as there seemed to be nothing I could do there.

*Note: This was before fathers became involved in the birthing process. This was the era when father's stayed in the waiting room and was told what it was after the baby was born.*

Being a novice at this new parenting thing, I left and went to the crusade, leading the singing with inspiring hymns and special music. The speaker gave a great salvation message! Several Japanese and Americans accepted. Christ and I did the personal work with four of them, leaving an hour later.

Ringing the hospital several times, there was only a recording stating they would be open again at 8:30am the next day. Another GI who was with me, suggested that I go home, and try calling again the next morning, as it was now after 1am. I went home and awoke early to drive to the hospital.

**Postscript** *Now I would advise all new fathers-to-be, "Stay at the hospital and do the waiting. Nothing is more important than being there to share that important moment with your wife and child! This action haunted me for several years, as my wife reminded me occasionally, "You weren't there." It seems that the birthing process speeded up after my departure, and our son, Elgin Jr. was born at 10 pm.*

I arrived early the next morning, (so I thought), and was greeted with the question, "Where have you been? We have had a new baby around here since 10 pm last night with no father. "Oh," I said, "I was told to come back this morning as the birth would take several hours, I tried calling but no one answered the phone. All I got was messages on the answering machine saying you opened again at 8:30 am. Therefore, I went home and came back this morning!" I was anxious to know what Dorothy would say, so I eased into her room. As I entered, she repeated the same question, but didn't labor over it. She was too eager to show me our new son! "Elgin Jr weighed in at 6 pounds," she said, "and is 18 inches long, and looks just like his father!" At that moment, the nurse brought the baby into the room; I noticed that he had his mother's coloring and my nose and eyes.

Words are never sufficient to describe the emotions that sweep through a man holding his first-born son. I was elated to see how perfectly formed he was and with those tiny toes and feet. I just held him, prayed, and thanked God for a safe delivery. Dorothy then filled me in on the details. About an hour after I left, last night, her labor speeded up and the doctor and nurse stayed with her the entire time, just talking and asking questions about our ministry.

She loves to chuckle at herself, as she tells this little story. She says, "I asked the Doctor, "How many patients could they accommodate and he said ninety." She then asked, "How many do you have now?" Knowing that she wasn't thinking too quickly while in labor, He said, "If we had 89 more, we would have ninety." After a second or two, Dorothy replied, "You mean I am the only patient here?" Yes, he replied and the first in-house patient. This made our son the first child born at the Adventist Hospital on the island.

Elgin was a sweet baby, extremely fair skinned at birth; but he grew well and within a few months developed a great tan like his old man. However, he had a nervous stomach that caused him to regurgitate much of his milk. If you bounced him, you were subjected to a milk shower. We were on guard, to keep him from being bounced or moved about after feeding times.

# Chapter 9

## Our Life with the Japanese

Our Japanese neighbors loved seeing the child and they would gather outside our little house to see how he was growing. The older women also wanted to see how Dorothy was caring for him. Since she didn't speak Japanese, they could not give her the instructions they desired to give. Due to Elgin Jr being nervous and jumpy, and regurgitating a portion of each feeding, the Doctor advised us to sleep him on his stomach after he was six weeks old. The locals sleep their babies only on their back.

One morning Dorothy laid the baby on his stomach in his crib, with the sliding doors open. Then she proceeded to go down into the kitchen to wash dishes. A few minutes later when checking on the baby, she found him on his back. She was so puzzled that she couldn't believe it "Perhaps I left him that way"; she thought and turned him on his stomach once more. Returning a second time, again, she found the baby once more on his back, and then realized that someone was slipping in and quietly turning the baby over.

When I came in that evening, she was overly excited that someone was turning the baby over whenever she left the room. I quietly went to our landlord to explain why the baby had to sleep on his stomach. Through a translator, they stated that in their culture, you never sleep a baby that way and some of the grandmothers were afraid we would kill the baby, so they were watching out for us. Rather than upset so many people, we never placed the baby on his stomach again. We felt it was more important that we become a part of the local community.

Our neighbors rallied around us and we hired a local girl to come and help with the laundry. The people were farmers, so they would placed fresh vegetables outside our door each morning and even left Dorothy Yogurtal (an orange flavored yogurt) for the first six weeks that she was breast-feeding. This helped us develop a wonderful relationship with the community, and made us feel a part of them.

Our first home in Okinawa was in the village of Kitinakagusuku. We entered via four steps up to a wooden gate leading into a bricked in square courtyard. The property owner's home was directly opposite the gate and ours was to the right with two empty sheds to the left. Each building had an 8-foot water tank, which collected water from the roof, and we boiled it before using or drinking it.

The Japanese homes were mostly wooden with red tiled roofs, which were safer to with stand typhoon-force winds. We were told that the houses were especially built to let the winds flow through rather than blow them away. There was an attached but outside chemical toilet. The honey bucket men would come and clean out the toilets every 3 months, there was no bathroom or washbasin. We went to the public bathhouse every other day for baths,

Each morning we would hear all the sliding doors opening as our neighbors prepared for the day. There were various sounds surrounding us. Children did the usual morning search for clothes and schoolbooks, and the usual complaints against eating breakfast.

The men would gather around a neutral water tank, brush their teeth, and shave in the mornings, while discussing the latest news. At first, we thought they were angry; however, we soon learned that they spoke in loud excited voices when discussing issues. The women kept busy doing house and field chores during the day. In the evenings, they would gather to hear the latest happenings in the village.

You may say that we were the big happening for quite a while. I am sure that they enjoyed watching our way of doing things, just as we enjoyed learning theirs. We learned to barter for everything at the outdoor markets and in the clothing shops. There were three prices, the American price, the outsider price, and the local village price. Gradually, they began to give us the local prices and we no longer had to remind them that we were "local." This also meant they were accepting us as part of their village.

Every good etiquette book advised us not to offend our hosts by refusing to eat what you were given. Dorothy did not like the strong green tea that they served constantly at all the homes. To be polite, at first she would drink it slowly them quickly shallow the remainder. The host, seeing her empty cup, would rush to refill it. Soon we both learned to slowly sip the tea, then the host would not hurry away to refill it. We also learned to use this method with food. If you disliked a particular dish, leave it on the plate and the host would not bring more of her precious delicacies to you. Food was expense and no one wanted to waste it.

Going to the Japanese Ofudo, (bathhouse) was a riot for us on the first visit. When we entered, they gave each adult a plastic bucket and a pan. There was one side for men and boys, and another for women and girls. Everyone brought his or her own toiletries and towels. The bathhouses were like huge swimming pools with a large hot pool in the center and taps all along the wall.

At first, I watched as the men filled their buckets with hot water and soaped themselves down. This they repeated it two or three times. Following suite, I soaped down, rinsed a bit, and then repeated the same. However, once I covered myself with soap, I assumed that you entered the big pool of hot water to rinse it off. As I stepped into the water, I heard a loud exclamation, in Japanese, oki –Sum-mi-oh, all around the room, the men rushed to assist me out of the pool. The manger came and tried explaining, that the large pool was only for soaking after you had washed under the taps and rinsed off all the soap. He would have to empty out the soapy water and reheat the entire pool due to the soap I had gotten in it.

That was quite a lesson, nevertheless, on repeat visits; the men would come and speak to me in their broken English. I would in turn use the Japanese that I learned on my first trip to the Island. Together, we would all work on learning to communicate with one another.

Dorothy and young Elgin did not have all the excitement that I had. The women gathered around her and assisted her and the baby. Therefore, she was able to ask questions and not make such a costly error.

I diligently maintained my language study each week. My goal was to give simple lessons without a translator before leaving the Island. Holding a conversation was not the issue; I could speak Japanese well; but religious language was much more difficult to present clearly. Each day I would add two or three new words to my vocabulary and practice the pronunciation repeatedly.

# Chapter 10

## Ministry to US Military

Two months after our arrival on the Island, Ron Rinnert left for the states for a year's furlough. We purchased his specially designed jeepney, that was an extended jeep with a white canopy top with "Light of the World Mission" written in black lettering on each side. This jeep was great advertising for the mission and us. It helped many people to recognize us all over the Island. The Quisenberrys' had one identical to it.

This was also during the time of segregation, and Black families were not well received into mixed congregations. We were not only well received, but were warmly embraced as one of their leaders. Both the Japanese and American personnel respected us and many approached us for advice and counseling. This seemed so strange to us, at first, then we recognized that they respected our position and calling upon our lives, regardless of our age.

One family in particular sought us out, after seeing us in the jeepney. One afternoon, when Elgin was returning home after classes in Naha, as he drove into our driveway an Afro-American couple pulled into the drive behind him. They jumped out of their car and ran up to greet him before he entered the house. "Hello there, they said, "We are the Buchanan's and we have noticed you around for two weeks. Today we saw you pass and decided to follow you and find out where you are located."

I invited them into the house and introduced them to my wife and child then we all sat down around our little Japanese table on the floor and talked. Robert and Mae Buchanan and their six children became a great part of our ministry, as supporters and prayer warriors.

Mae had a wonderful gift as a Bible teacher and singer. Having a large family kept her busy but she was faithful to the church, the Bible studies, and later, the outreach to the Black Servicemen on Four Corners. This family became our closest friends for three years and they opened their home to us. From their home, we began a work among Afro-American Service Personnel and their families.

Two other families that we should mention were the Lee family and the Jones family. Lola Lee and her three children attended church every Sunday afternoon and she also held a weekly Bible study in her home near gate three. The big Quonset huts that many GI families had were very roomy and air-conditioned so the people would attend them more readily than they would attend the mission that was not air-conditioned.

The Jones family was gifted in hospitality and Charles Jones was an awesome Sunday school teacher. He volunteered to assist Dorothy in the Children's church and took over that ministry when we left for furlough. His wife was a melt in your mouth, soul-food cook. She prepared many scrumptious dinners for us, all our missionaries, and even invited our Japanese staff during the holidays.

Food for the missionaries on the island was limited to what we could purchase at a place in Naha called, "Black Market Alley." It was a back street market where the Japanese sold the food that was, *"Donated by the people of the USA, not for resale."* They did not use such products as flour, meal, oatmeal, and catsup. They mostly used rice, noodles, Spam, chicken, and fish. Therefore, they sold the rest to earn cash dollars.

Sometimes, the visiting single servicemen would bring foods that they missed from home, for us to prepare. Napoleon Weaver, a newly arrived marine joined our ministry. Napoleon was one of Dorothy's former pupils at Carver High School, and a pastor's son. He also shared that he had joined the Marines after hearing Elgin share his testimony in his home church. He was an excellent example of God preserving and protecting young people, if they desired to remain faithful in their walk. He worked with the Bible study group' witnessed on the streets; and visited with us often. He even took us on a full tour of the Island before he left for home.

Two other young men, (both white) through whom we were blessed above measure, were Grant Ray, a bright Redhead from Indiana. He spoke often of his wife Lois and his family back home. We became their family and maintained an open door for them when they needed fellowship.

Grant was an outstanding church worker and drove the jeep that seated eight persons to special outreaches. He maintained the sound equipment and helped store it each week. When home on furlough in

1970, we were blessed to visit Grant, Lois, and their five children. Lois was confined to a wheelchair, due to Multiple Sclerosis. Her children were gladly ministering to her needs. It was a joy to see how God was using this family during this crisis to show love and gentleness. We thank God for Grant and his lovely wife for those many years they spent praying for us.

The other young man was, Marshal Ruth. Marshall accepted Christ in our Bible study and I baptized him in a mountain stream during a men's retreat in the North of the Island. He received a call to ministry and returned to California to enter school. When we arrived back in California on furlough, he was completing his training and deputation. Dorothy and I were delighted to participate in his commissioning service. In 1964, He went out as a single man to South Korea, later he married Sandy, and they served in Korea together. Today, they are working with Korean churches, here in America.

# Chapter 11

## (OCS) Okinawa Christian School Opens

The year before our arrival, a group of missionaries organized a Christian school for missionary's children. They had immense plans and hopes for the school and knowing Dorothy was a teacher, they had looked forward to her arrival. Now Dorothy on the other hand, had doubts about going back to work as a teacher. "I came do missionary work in the villages, not teach school, again," she said to me at home. Being the softhearted person she was, as they became more desperate, she began to feel the pull towards helping where needed most.

In May, 1960, the registration for "Okinawa Christian School was drawn up by the board, chaired by Carl Johnson, Director of *Christians in Action Missions* on the island, who was the principal of the school. As the school opening grew closer, the board was told that they required one more teacher with a college degree and teacher's certificate, before the school qualified for a permit.

When Carl approached us concerning Dorothy teaching at the school, I left it up to her. We had a three-month-old son and she could stay home with him. She also knew that the baby would be six months old when school opened in September. In the meanwhile, Dorothy realized that a missionary was "One fulfilling a special call from God to fulfill a particular job, or mission," therefore, teaching, whether it was the Bible or secular classes to the children, was a necessary mission. Seeing the urgent need, she joyfully volunteered to be the registered teacher. Through this gesture, the school now had a qualified teacher for the upper grades 5-8.

Miss Ann Jones was the Secretary; and the five teachers were: Mrs. Austin-grade - one; Mrs. Eva Johnson - grade two; Mrs. Chassell - grades three and Mrs. Jackson - grade four; and Dorothy - Grades 5; 6;7; 8; & special students(students who weren't conversant in English). As you may note, Dorothy had her hands full. She managed to teach those classes well. One of her students, who could not speak English upon his arrival, David Feng, graduated from Drexel University in Philadelphia, and has worked as a Ford Motor Co Executive for 35 years.

She devised methods of teaching several subjects together such as English, Spelling, and Math. When I visited the school, or arrived early, I noticed that the children were well behaved and orderly. They respected her and several times, we had all of them over for holiday celebration or class picnics.

Our morning routine was to await the arrival of the child minder, Chizuko, a college student from the local village; have prayer, then, I would drop my wife off and go to the mission where I taught three Bible classes for the Japanese Bible School via a translator.

Okinawa Christian School was located in two three-roomed Quonset huts at old Camp Kue near the Naval Hospital, right on the ocean. People seeing that area today would never know that the government of Japan reclaimed the present area three miles into the sea. Several regions are like that. Our house had overlooked Buckner Bay, today it is four to five miles from the ocean. Many of the present roads and hotels have been built after the Islands reverted to Japan in the 1970s.

There were five classrooms, with the office in the center of the second one. From these humble beginnings, grew what is now a multi-million dollar campus in Okinawa City with over 1500 students. The original teachers were paid only $125 per month, with Dorothy getting $50 dollars extra for having a fully qualified license, along with having multiple classes.

All of Dorothy's students, except three, who were already Christians, accepted Christ while in her classes. Each morning she held fifteen minutes of devotions and prayer with them and presented a life application. After the first six months, many of them also begin attending our Junior Church at Kitanakigusuku, "Light of the World Church." Of course Dorothy decided since the ranged in age from 10-15, they were old enough to be put to work, as her assistants. She had the junior church set up in three parts. The singing and devotional; a flannel graph missionary story; and a short film strip. The film stripes were from Kadena Chapel and we had brought the flannel graph boards and pictures with us from California. The junior church grew to over ninety in number by the time we returned home for furlough in 1964.

A few new students were added, but most of the regulars remained at OCS throughout our time there. We met and became good friends with many of the parents. Most were civilian workers with the US military from the Philippines, Guam, Hawaii, USA, and main land Japan. For most, except the missionary children, English was their second language. The parents encouraged and pushed their children as they studied English and Math subjects, in order to improve their chances to attend schools and colleges in America.

**Making higher education my goal:** During this time, on the Island, I signed up for courses at the University of Maryland extension classes on Kadena Air Force Base, being a veteran; those privileges were open to me. For two or three nights each week, I attended English, Japanese, and Psychology classes. Bible study courses were not offered, or I would have taken them also. I felt that those classes would help me to improve my knowledge of languages and people. They were just the beginning as I later studied at London Bible College and the International Bible College in Florida.

Later, I also began to help teach English at the University of the Ryukus. It was called the Fisherman's Club, and there were about eighty students in the one class. Another missionary had started the class, but when he was preparing to leave, I was approached to carry on the ministry. It was a very rewarding ministry as these young men and women were slated to become the business leaders of the future.

They were eager to ask questions and they requested that we use the American Standard Bible as their English book. Of course, I had to add an English Dictionary to their list but this was a wonderful evangelizing tool. It also led to many religious discussions for the group, sometimes I had to learn how to be diplomatic in my approach to their ancient Shinto faith and explain why we did not "worship the dead." The Bible came alive in this type of setting for you could see II Cor.8 -jump out at you as you read about food offered to idols and honoring the dead.

# Chapter 12

## The Idol Burning Ceremony

Within four months of our arrival on the Island, Ron Rinnert returned home on furlough. The Quisenberrys family followed him two months later. This left only the Johnson's and the Taylors to carry on the ministry. Carl and Eva Johnson had their hands full, with both working at OCS and Pastoring in another village.

We were in charge of the Kitanakigusuku headquarters church and all the English services. I was the main Pastor each Sunday, with Dorothy teaching and supervising the Children's ministry. Ron Rinnert and his new bride, Elaine arrived from Long Beach in March 1961.

The Johnson Family was great friends' and they encouraged us to be all that we could be in our ministry. They met with us often, and visit in our home. We could also return the favor at anytime. They were experienced parents with 3 children, Gary 8, Janet, 5, and Sharon, 3. We could ask them our questions on parenting and exchange ideas. It was an awesome time that we shared. We can never thank them enough for being there along side us at this marvelous time of growth. This experience forced us to develop our leadership and people-to-people skills and anchored us deeply for the ministry of Pastoring God's flock, anywhere in the World.

There were many Missionaries on the Island, and many of them received us well. We became good friends with Rev and Mrs. Merrill Bennett of the Nazarene church; the Shepherds of the Assemblies of God; and several Japanese Pastors. Later I joined the local Pastoral Association and met many of the National Pastors.

Shinto worship is centered around the offering of food on a "Budsidon (a God Shelf) `'" to ones dead ancestors. If you did not follow the traditions, they believed "the Gods would punish you." This shelf was the centerpiece in living rooms, usually made of beautiful polished wood. Small tablets containing the names of the dead are place in order of their place in the family. Blue and gold bowls of incense and food are placed on the shelves in front of the tablets. Some Christians continued to put food on the God shelf rather than destroy it, out of fear of what would happen.

On Sundays, I would preach the Sunday services with Bro. Shinyu Kuniyoshi standing on a box beside to me. This was quite a remarkable sight each week, as he would copy my gestures and emphasis all the same points as we shared together in both English and Japanese. Soon we were able to carry on very smoothly without pausing for clarification. In the early days, sometimes we went over the message on Saturdays to clarify many English words to Him. Later, he said, I know you now, so I can follow quite rapidly with the Japanese. This was a great way for me to learn the Japanese too, for I could anticipate when to begin or end, without long pauses.

The entire Kuniyoshi family would come to the services to support their son and brother; however, many of them were not Christians. One Sunday, his father came forward and received Christ, what a rejoicing there was among the church members. They knew that we had prayed for family members to find Christ. Our national pastor had prayed and claimed his family according to Acts 16: 31 for over ten years.

We led Papa Kuniyoshi in the sinner's prayer; his son hugged him and prayed in Japanese. Each week he faithfully attended Bible classes. He began to go into many villages and pass out Gospel tracts. He would ride his bicycle or go by bus to rural areas just to see that they received the Word.

After six months of study, Papa Kuniyoshi approached his son and me, stating, "I really must removed and destroy the Idols in my home! Can I bring them here and burn them in the mission fireplace?" This was a shock to the other Christians in the room. They began to say the usual things, Oh, please, wait a while! Think about this; do not offend your grandmother! *Grandmothers were the ones in charge of the "God shelf."* "I have already spoken to my mother and grandmother about this," he said, and they agree that we must destroy our idols."

Bro Kuniyoshi took his father home and arranged for them to have an idol burning ceremony the following Wednesday morning. Many church members came to see what he would do. There was hardly room enough for all the people. As they watched, Papa Kuniyoshi picked up a big metal bucket, took the tablets with the names of the dead, along with the beautiful pottery bowls for the food, and broke them into pieces with a hammer.

His next step was to throw them into the fireplace on top of wood that had been prepared for burning. He, his wife, and his mother set fire to the tablets together, while repeating over and over, Joshua 24:15, "As for me and my house, we shall serve the Lord (God). I led a prayer over them in the name of the Father; Son; and Holy Spirit, while committing the idols to the flames, never to worship them again. They also read the Ten Commandments from Exodus 20:1-18, emphasizing the passage, "Thou shall have no other God before me."

People wept and danced around the room as we all began to bind away the attacks of Satan upon this family as they took this step of faith! For a number of years we had slides of the ceremony and showed them across the USA, but now they seem to be lost.

# Chapter 13

## A second Idol burning!

Over the next three months, the Kuniyoshi family grew in the Lord and witnessed of God's goodness among their neighbors. They invited many to church and told them of how they had gotten rid of the idols in their home. Their next door neighbor watched out the window each morning as Papa Kuniyoshi went to the fields with his hoe draped over his shoulder; his "o'bento (lunch); and singing Christian songs in Japanese. One morning he decided to talk to Papa about his new faith, and went out and met him on the way home.

After hearing what God had done in his life, the neighbor said, I want the God that you have! Can I receive Him too, like you? Bro Kuniyoshi quietly read several scriptures to him and prayed for him to receive Christ.

A few weeks later, we again had an idol burning ceremony in the hall at the church. Again, people began to pronounce doom and gloom upon the family. The following week, we held a baptismal service and baptized the two families.

Things went along well for both families. Suddenly, two months later, the neighbor had stayed home from work with his 2-year-old daughter, who was ill with a high fever. As he went to awaken her to give her water, he found her very cold and not breathing. After several minutes and many shakes with no response, he picked the child up and ran next door to Papa K's house. "My child has died, he cried, "The people will think it's because I became a Christian and burned the idols. What can we do?

Papa K said he had just read about the death of Lazarus, and about Jesus raising him from the dead. He said I believe he can do the same with this child! He took the child and laying her on the floor began to prayer for her asking Jesus to raise her up as He had raised Lazarus, for a testimony before the people.

By this time, many people had gather around because of the commotion, as Japanese homes were built close and the entire group of four front doors slide open during the day. Remember these were young Christians and they did not know much about healing and certainly had not heard of anyone rising from the dead. They just believed God for what was in the Bible! As they closed the prayer, they heard a small cough, and then another and another, the child was alive!

People from all around the village ran to see the child who had been raised from the dead! The family became faithful believers; and a church was built in their village; and their elder son became a Minister of the Gospel. He is now pastoring in the same village.

# Chapter 14

## The Koza Fellowship Center

Due to the areas where Americans gathered being segregated, there was little or no ministry being done among the Black servicemen in an area called "Four Corners" We are talking of a Island with several hundred missionaries working only with GI's. Having always been with a mixed group, we began to inquire why there were so few Blacks in all the various ministries and why there was no work in the "Four Corners" area. Things became quiet and cool.

The same excuse was offered repeatedly, "God has not called us to that area of ministry. How persons could justify traveling thousands of miles to win the "lost" Japanese and White servicemen, but not ever feel called to Black Servicemen seems very out of step with Scripture. We worked well together as long as we stayed clear of the "Ghetto"

I suggested that we all stay together and work the Four Corners area the same as we had done in all the others. There was much opposition. You go! They are your people!

Dorothy and I decided we must go and set up an outreach among the Blacks. Several male missionaries agreed to join us as long as their wives did not have to attend. This hurt us very much, for it was as though it was OK for "White servicemen" to make passes or say anything they pleased, but somehow it was unacceptable for others to do the same.

We rented a former brothel house and redecorated it with more sober colors, and named it *The Koza Fellowship Center.* It was divided into three sections; the reception and game room; a prayer, and chapel, to allow it to function like the one in Oceanside where I had been saved. There would be a fellowship time with refreshments in the recreation area, then at 8: pm each night, the musician played Christian songs in the partitioned off chapel. The staff personally invited any servicemen present to join them in singing around the piano. Those who were interested could go into the chapel, those who did not could still hear the songs and salvation message sitting out in the recreational area.

Each evening, one person would casually share their testimony and another gave a short salvation message. The men followed those who came forward for prayer up on their base later in the week. It was important that the men were contacted within two days of their conversion.

We had many GIs coming each week to the center and the group began to grow so much so that it was suggested that we should plan a church service twice monthly on Sunday afternoons. However, I felt that would cause a greater division among the races. So we continued to fellowship at the Mission on Sunday afternoons.

You must remember we were the only Black missionaries to the orient at this time. You couldn't say "Go and Fellowship with your own people" as we have been told many times since then, but here there were no other of our kind as our peers. Fellowship with young converts was not the same as fellowshipping with your peers of seasoned maturity in Christ.

By this time, we received word that Bill and Adeline Quisenberry and family had decided not to return to the Island, but were transferring to Brazil, South America. This was a real shock for us. They had been Mom and Pop to all of us regardless of our race or origin. The Chinese; Japanese; Philippinos Blacks; Whites and Browns; we had been well received by of them.

In the summer of 1962, another missionary and his family returned to Okinawa from Japan. Gary Woods had worked with our team as a GI just as I had. He had gone to Japan for two years language school and to meet his Japanese wife's parents. Gary and Holly Woods and their four children, were great additions to the team. Holly worked well with the women and was a wonderful translator in English and Japanese.

Gradually, since there were more workers, I asked that we all share the pulpit duties at the main mission. Slowly, we again started rotating the pulpit duties on Sunday mornings. This now meant that I was I was only sharing every four weeks, with Carl Johnson; Ron Rinnert and Gary Woods filling in the other Sundays.

This gave me more time at Koza Fellowship Center and allowed us to begin a village film ministry around the Island. Dorothy and I worked with a convert, Doug Harris, who supervised the Kadena Air Force Base Film Library. He told us of the many 16mm Moody Science Films in the

Japanese Language that were available to us if we had a 16mm projector. As civilians, we could check out films, but not the projectors or other equipment.

There were several ministry support groups on the Island, who donated equipment and funds for special projects. One of these was, *Okinawa for Christ*, led by a Navy Officer with the Seabees, Commander Scot Sprague. We approached them with an appeal for a 16mm projector and 400-watt generator, for a mission film ministry.

Praise God, their board accepted the challenge and they presented the projector and generator to the mission in the early spring of 1962. Dorothy, Mitsako, Pastor Kuniyoshi, and I covered at least three villages each month. We would have a time of singing hymns in Japanese, one very short testimony, and show the film. The films themselves had a Gospel message so those who wanted to know more about Jesus went to the councilors afterwards.

We covered most of the villages around the Island two or more times and even went to one of the other Islands in the Ryukus chain. Praise God, today each of those villages have at least one Christian Church. This was just one method that God gave us to reach the Japanese people. We also spent many hours passing out tracts donated by Every Home Crusade, a movement that was popular in the 1960s.

# Chapter 15

## The House Dedicated to the Dead in Awase

Our first move was due to our property owner buying three huge breeding sows and putting them in the small shed opposite our front door. We were shocked that anyone would do such a thing. Every time they cleaned out the pens, the odor was unbearable. Having no say in how the property could be used, we felt we must move away from the stench. A missionary family was leaving on furlough, and their house was available to rent. We drove to Toguchi to view it and saw that there were no close neighbors to cause us to have to move again. We rented the house and moved the following weekend. We had spoken to the former property owner and he had approved our moving at anytime.

The next house was on the edge of the village of Toguchi, surrounded by rice and sugar cane. The missionaries had instructed us to keep the doors closed between the lean-to kitchen and the rest of the house. The house had two bedrooms and large sitting room, a wrap around walkway, and a kitchen addition with a lean-to roof.

When we moved into the house, things were quiet as it was early afternoon. That night, we could hear a slight occasional noise. We were use to lizards on the ceilings, birds on top of the roof, and other similar noises, after all we were on a small island in the great Pacific Ocean. As the fall approached, the ceiling noises increased, as the field mice search for a warm place for the winter. They could not enter the house as long as we kept the door closed from the kitchen. We would lie in bed and hear sounds like rats playing baseball across our ceiling!

Having a young child, we were afraid that the rats might bit him so we tried getting the rats exterminated. It seemed that as soon as we got rid of five, eight would take their place.

Once again, we were house hunting. We were going to be sure that the next house had no nocturnal visitors!

Lastly, we rented a house from a Japanese war widow. Her husband had been killed in the battle of Iwo Jima, and she showed us photos of him upon her Budsidon (godshelf) Having been shown all of her objects before renting the house, we had assumed that she would take them with her when she moved from the house.

On the day of our move, several persons came and helped us. The Buchanan's were especially involved. They helped us move and arrange our furniture. She also noticed the things on the godshelf were still there. We said we would contact the owner, and ask her to come and take them. Naturally, we assumed that we had rented the total house, so why would she leave her things there.

That evening I had, a meeting at the church, Dorothy and Elgin Jr, three, were left finishing the unpacking and then, off to bed. Children are very sensitive to changes and Elgin Jr. became fretful and refused to let his mother out of his sight. At bedtime, she sat near his bed and rocked him to sleep.

After settling the child, Dorothy began to feel a presence in the house, yet no one was there. Preparing for bed, she went throughout the house turning off the lights. As she switched off the sitting room light, the photos over the Budsadon (god shelf) began to glow larger and larger in the dark. Not having had this experience before, she just shrugged her shoulders and thought she was Imagining things. As she turned off the last light to climb into bed, she said it was as someone was standing besides her watching her every move. She prayed and bound the spirit of fear and evil away in the name of Jesus, and turned the lights back on in both our room and the sitting room.

When I arrived home an hour later, I thought she was still working on the unpacking, with so many lights. However, as I entered the house, I also felt a strange and clammy presence. Dorothy upon hearing my arrival met me at the door, sharing the happenings of the evening. We immediately knelt and prayed in each room and bound the spirits from the house, reading aloud from Psalms 91.

# Chapter 16

## The "gods" in a box

The next morning, Dorothy gathered all the "gods" (note the small "g") from the god shelf; wrapped them nicely; and placed them carefully in one of the packing cases we had used in moving. Mae Buchanan returned to assist her, and stated that the house felt better today than it did yesterday. She stated how felt clammy and cold the she had felt while helping us the day before but did not want to frighten us about our house. We then explain what had happened the night before. Mae prayed for the house all over again.

When our property-owner came to collect her rent, she bowed to the "god shelf" upon entering the house, not noticing it was no longer there. Looking up, she screamed and began praying very quickly in Japanese; turned and ran down the road. We were not sure what had offended her; somehow, we knew she was upset over the gods no longer being where she left them.

She soon returned with a Buddhists Priest. He asked Dorothy in English, "Where are the Budsadon articles?" Dorothy walked to the back closet and showed him the box. He stated that we had offended the widow woman by putting her "gods" in a box. She wanted them returned to the shelf. Dorothy then told him that as Christian missionaries, we would not have idols on our shelf nor did we want to keep them in our house. She would have to take the idols with her, or we would have to find another place to live.

The lady said she needed the money, and Okinawans could not afford the present rent. The Priest had a little prayer ceremony with her and entreating their gods not to be angry, set a good day to move the "gods" by the Zodiac calendar. He then announced the day that was lucky and asked if I could please keep the items until that time. He also requested that we keep them in the front living room closet as that was more pleasing.

This was just one of many encounters we had with this particular landlord, so we decided to seek for another place soon. We shared this incident with our donors letting them know about the situation. We also announced that we would probably have to move due to the woman being offended by her gods being put in a box.

# Chapter 17

## The Miracle House in Shimabuku

We could not close this section without mentioning the miracle God worked for us in Shimabuku. After having been on the Island for fourteen months, we had moved three times due to unforeseen issues.

One Wednesday after work, Dorothy noticed a "For Sale" sign on a 2-bedroomed brick house in Shimibuku. This was unusual as most homes were own by the Japanese and they rented them to the Americans excepting to move into them themselves after the Americans were gone. We passed that way often, and it was near the Mission. " Honey, she began, why don't we check and see what they are asking for that house" Knowing that we didn't have any extra funds for a good down payment even, I just said, "Maybe one of these days, but not right now." After a week of passing that sign, I quietly stopped to check on the asking price.

An American Air Force Major's wife answered the door. She stated that her husband was on a mission to Vietnam (before the war) and she now had a house available on base. They wanted $3500 for the house. As we talked, I felt led to ask if she would accept half down and monthly payments for the remaining balance. She said she would need to ask her husband, but felt they could arrange that. She also felt that her husband, being a committed Christian would want to help a missionary as much as possible.

That evening I had good news for my wife, she was so elated that I did not want to burst her bubble by saying, only one problem; we do not have the $1500 for the down payment! The next morning, Dorothy rose bright and early, wrote a short prayer letter, and put it in envelopes for me to mail out on my way to the Mission. She put photos of the area and of the house. When she had taken them, I did not know, but it was where we held baptismal services. She had hoped that I would finally agree to check on the house.

On the tenth of the following month, our check arrived with more than enough funds to meet the down payment plus a bit more to cover furniture and moving expenses. Doctor Dalton had sent the $1500 and two other people had given a $100. The extra also allowed us to paint the inside and fix up Elgin Jr's room.

We had a beautiful view of the Buckner Bay and White Beach, with awesome sunsets across the water. Today, high-rise buildings surround the house and the reclamation project by the government has pushed the sea out for over five miles.

It was in Shimabuku that a lovely Christian woman joined our family, Mitsako Mayagi. She worked with the Nazarene missionaries and they highly recommended her as a house cleaner and child minder. Dorothy was still teaching and our former house cleaner had not been able to move, as she was a local college student.

Mitsako was having struggles at home, as her family were not believers. We agreed to pay her the same as we had paid the former housekeeper even though she would live in, as she needed the funds to help her family. She was especially sweet and patient with our son, Elgin Jr. He grew to love her and missed her terribly when she visited her parents every other weekend.

Mitsako had an unusual sickness; Narcolepsy She always says it was caused by being dropped on her head as a baby. It was amazing to watch her, whenever she felt sleepy, she would pause whatever she was doing and stand up against the wall. Then the next thing we knew, she was asleep. Young Elgin would go and shake her and try to wake her up, but he soon learned that she would not stay a sleep for long. It was more like a nodding off, and then she would be wide-awake again.

These "spells" were not long nor were they debilitating to her. She had been in many prayer sessions over this but God had not delivered her of it. We had several prayer sessions and God did answer in allowing the spells to become shorter in duration and less often. After we left the Island, she married a Christian worker from Osaka and moved away, now she has a lovely son of her own. We thank God for sending Mitsako to our home and the wonderful way in which she assisted us while there.

After moving to Shimabuku, we increased our film ministry. In this ministry, we took 16mm Moody Science films translated in Japanese to many villages. Mitsako Shimagiri was the translator, traveling with Dorothy, Elgin Jr, and myself most nights. We took Elgin Jr along just for the fun of being with Mom and Dad. We hated to leave him behind in the evenings since we were both away during the day.

# Chapter 18

## God's Bountiful Provision

Two very important events that we do not want to over look were two special ways in which God provided for us in miraculous ways. We were totally dependant upon God's provision by faith; ten thousand miles from home; and living among non-believers. As missionaries trying to show the wonderful attributes of Jesus and his love for the world, we never dishonored our Lord by complaining over what we did not have. Dorothy and I never asked for money or food on the Island. We prayed for them and if they did not come, we assumed God was working it out according to his own will, not ours.

The first Instance was in the fall of 1962; I had gone to the post office for our check and upon opening it, could not believe my eyes. It was only $28! Thinking that perhaps this was something extra rather than our entire months check, I read the fine print; this really was our funds for the month!

Quietly I prayed and went through my usual routine. That evening, Dorothy enquired, "Did our check come? I thought it would have been here today" I simply handed her the envelope and let her see the check for herself.

By now, you know what a great gal I married. She looked at that check and did not bat an eye, but went on to say, "We have our rent, $25 and electricity, $2 and propane gas$1, it seems that God plans to feed us another way! This was so classic Dorothy; that I just hugged her and said, "I guess he does Honey." I was still concerned that we would not have sufficient to care for the baby for the month. Dorothy's pay at OCS barely covered our car and petrol bills so we still needed at least another $150 for food. We did not have surplus as we were just managing from month to month.

We attended our usual with weekly Bible studies and teaching classes. On the Wednesday evening as we were parking our car at the Bible study, Jenny Pollard, a recent convert whom Dorothy had led to Christ, approached us. "Please leave your car unlocked, she continued, I have some things at my house that I need to bring back and put in it for you. "

Obeying, we left it and proceeded to carry on with the evening. After saying our goodbye, we opened the car door and low and behold, the rear seat was filled to the ceiling with American foodstuffs! There were all the things we could not buy even if we had the money. We were humbled as we realize that God had answered in the most miraculous way.

When Dorothy called Jennie the next day, she informed us that the exterminators had come to her house and she had emptied out the cupboards. As she started to put the food back into the cupboards, the Lord told her, "Don't put this all back. You are getting short (term used when nearing the time to leave) take this food and give it to the Taylors tonight." She said I wanted to obey the Lord, so, my husband brought it to you."

We drove over and personally thanked her and her husband for their gift. This was our first time visiting with Al, as he was always working on his day job or at the NCO Club, evenings. Today, they are both serving God as volunteers at an intercity mission in Las Vegas, NV. Later that week we also shared this experience in our English service. Sometimes our needs are not money, and God has His way of supplying just what we need.

The second occasion was similar; we ran short of funds ten days before the end of the month. There was no way we could raise funds, except tell everyone we did not get enough money this month to meet our needs.

Being missionaries; working with new converts; how could be say to them, "This Great; Wonderful; and Powerful God we have been telling you about is not taking care of us and is letting us starve. Some situations are best kept to ones self and prayed about in private. We knew it was not God but some of God's people who were not being faithful in their faith promises to us.

*Writer's note: Later we learned that Dr. Dalton and another donor had responded to a special emergency in the US and did not send that month. They had no way of knowing that we had so few donors. However, we always knew that our dependence was on God's supply not mans.*

The following Sunday morning, we had used everything we had except a small box of rice. In the afternoon, Dorothy who was expecting our son, Willis, said she should stay and rest instead of attending the afternoon service. I jokingly said, I'd be home in time for that big dinner you are fixing, and started out the door.

Dorothy coming outside to wave me off, said, 'I'll have the rice soup ready." As she stood waving me off, a US Army Sergeant's Japanese wife down the hill, begin waving back. Not seeing me take off, she thought Dorothy was waving at her. Coming up the hill, she asked, "Dorothy, do you know anything about cleaning fish?"

Need I tell you more? Dorothy had grown up in the fish business; so immediately answered, yes. The lady, Suzi explained that her husband and his friends had been deep-sea fishing on the weekend. Today they had returned with a huge tub of various types of fish. She did not know how to clean them or what she should do with them.

"If you can clean a few of them or show me how, then you can have all the rest," she continued. Dorothy went down the hill, and showed her how to clean; crab; red snapper; and marlins. They then brought the tub with the remaining large fish and crabs, up to our house. Now Dorothy proceeded to clean enough crab and fish for dinner and filled the refrigerator with the rest.

My wife always says she wishes there was a way you could hide the smell of fish cooking. She was just going to put rice on my plate and then pull out the fish as a great surprise! It was a great surprise to see what had happened while I was away.

This was also a testimony to us of how God will use many means to provide for his own. This family had been friendly, but they were not believers, but afterwards, we were good neighbors and saw them often for the remainder of our stay.

We cooked every recipe we knew using crabs, squid, and various fish for ten days. We even gave fish to other missionaries and nationals at the mission. It was as if Jesus' miracle when he fed the 5,000, there was more than enough.

# Chapter 19

## Our Second Son Arrives Two Months Premature!

Shortly after moving, we discovered that we were expecting again, after almost four years. We wanted a child to be a playmate for Elgin, but that had not happened sooner, due to a hormone imbalance that developed after a miscarriage. Now we were looking forward to a new addition to the family.

On the evening of October 25, 1963, our film team was going to a distant village Dorothy who was seven months pregnant decided she felt too tired to go with us. Being that she still had two months before the baby was due, we were pleased that she had decided to stay behind She was teaching everyday and arrangements had been made for a replacement teacher to come the following month so she could go on leave.

Upon completing services and putting up all the equipment, I drove home around 10pm. We lived only a mile from the mission, in Shimibuku. Upon entering the house, Dorothy said, Honey, I have been feeling very strange tonight, but I do not know what it is. As I began to undress, she made a gesture to get out of bed; in so doing, a pain hit her suddenly and I knew we were in trouble. Immediately, I re buttoned my shirt, drove to the mission to get Mitsuko, whom I had just dropped off, returned home, put Dorothy in the back seat, and immediately headed for the Hospital.

This time, I was really sweating it out; and praying all the way. First, I was concerned about Dorothy because it was much too soon. Next, I was frightened for the baby, few seven-month babies survived. During the drive, the contractions intensified and can closer and closer together! We arrived at the hospital at 1am and at 1:20am on the morning of the 26th, I heard the child cry. Therefore, you can see how quickly he arrived.

Willis Victor Taylor weighed in at 5pounds. 1oz. During this time, the Okinawan hospitals were in a transition. American personnel were being replaced by nationals and they had no incubator. The Doctor said they would have to keep him if he lost 1oz, but he must have heard them, for when it was time to go home three days later, he had put on 2oz. We were relieved not to leave the baby at the hospital; however, two weeks later, we almost regretted that decision. For you see, after taking him home, the child developed severe breathing difficulties and we had to make continual trips back to the hospital with him. They had nothing to offer us for such a small premature baby.

Later we learned that his breathing problems all stemmed from the lack of incubation at the time of birth. The child had under developed bronchial tubes that cause considerable distress in breathing. In our home, we had to keep the child upright at all times as well as try to keep him propped up on pillows; when we laid him down, he would turn blue and begin gasping for air.

Another issue was feeding. He could not digest breast milk or cow's milk. Everywhere milk touched his skin; he peeled and developed huge blisters. The Japanese Doctors had not seen anything like it before and the Army Doctors said they could not treat him since we were civilians

This caused Dorothy much distress as the mother watching the child's condition worsen, so much so that the stress produced a form of asthma in her. This caused me to feel more desperate for a solution to this urgent crisis within my own household. As the days passed, I wrote, called, and even sent short-waved radio messages to our Long Beach Office, trying to explain our critical situation. I told them several times, that we would have to bring the child home for treatment, as none was available on the island.

We also informed them that the only civilian airlines on the Island traveling between Okinawa and the USA, USOA was closing down and there was no way we could travel by ship with such a sick infant. It would take three days by plane or it would take thirty-six days by ship.

At first, the letter of the law was applied by our mission; all missionaries were required to stay on the field for a minimum of four years. Our four years would not be up until the end of January since that was when we arrived in Japan.

Finally, I had to insist that we must leave on December 20 since that was the last economical flight out and we had no other choice. I know this does not seem important to some of you, but it was of great importance to us and our circumstances at that time. It also taught us a lesson in GRACE, for we saw God's hand upon this situation in such a strong way, that we had to take a stand for what was a life and death issue! We had to take that Dec 20 flight or our child would die!

We proceeded to sell the house and gave most of our furnishings to the Mission and Pastor Kuniyoshi. There was not time to try selling things and this was urgent. On December 20, 1963, we flew home to the US for our first furlough. We were met by our President and Vice President. There was not the usual welcome by all the staff after a missionary had served a term on the field.

We must say that we were not handled delicately, and it almost caused us to leave the mission at that time. In fact, several other options by other groups were offered us. God would not let us give up on all we had worked so hard for over the past five or six years. I had started with this organization from its inception, and I was determined to stay. We appealed to the board, which met after church the next day. Upon showing Willis to them, they saw the critical and delicate state of the child. Over three-fourths of his body was covered with red blisters and peeling skin. Recognizing the seriousness of our situation, they accepted our early return, and voted in our favor.

That same afternoon, we took Willis to his namesake Doctor Willis Dalton. He took one look at the child and diagnosed the problem. He is a milk allergy baby! Here I have many soy samples and I will give him some antibiotics to fight that infection. Speaking of relief, we felt happy to know what was the cause of his illness. He gave us a few medications for our trip, since we were flying home to Texas for Christmas, then he gave the child two injections and said for us to bring him in for more injection when we returned from Texas.

Folks, there must be a message in there somewhere. The man whom we had named the child in honor of was also the person who saved his life. We were all named by God and made in his image? Then he had to come and rescue us? Willis was rescued twice by a man, and twice by a God Man—Jesus

We flew home to Texas to visit family and friends for the Holidays. Upon our arrival in Dallas, it snowed. Elgin Jr, age four, had grown up in the tropics and had never seen snow before, so he said, "Oh mother, look someone has defrosted a big refrigerator and poured ice all over the airport." This was a learning opportunity for us to explain about snow, as we scooped some up and showed him the difference between actual fluffy powdery snow from the heavens and frozen ice.

Our trip to Texas was tremendously refreshing. We renewed our relationship with older family members and introduced ourselves to many new ones. It was good to be with Dorothy's father in the Fish Market and share with him our progress. He was delighted to see how God had blessed and kept us during our ministry in Japan. He drove me around to buy a car for our return trip to California, and we had a relaxing time of fellowship.

We traveled for two weeks, between Dallas; Waco; Pelham and Leona; Texas. My maternal grandmother, Ada Chambers aged 80 lived in Leona. I wanted her to meet my wife and see the boys before she passed on. Even though she later lived to be 115, many of my family had lived over 100 years. My paternal grandfather had lived to be 105 and died in a house fire in Austin, Texas. He had been the longest serving Methodist preacher in Texas in 1951.

# Chapter 20

## The return to California

In January 1964, we returned to California to enter the missionary refresher course. There were four families and five single missionaries in the course. It was the usual classes, with a baby sitter taking care of the younger children in the nursery. The wives only attended in the mornings, but the husbands and singles had either more classes or local outreach in the afternoons.

This time was profitable to us; we met many co-laborers from various fields around the world and were also available to deputize on weekends and some weekdays. Again, I was put in charge of much of the outreach and some Radio ministry. Bro Lee and Frank shared the latest letters from the missionaries, and then I would bring in the reports from the street meetings, house to house witnessing, and follow up on new converts.

We really developed an exciting teamwork among ourselves, as we would choose a particular area of Los Angeles to evangelize then announce that we would report on the results next week. Many Radio listeners would come and join us when the outreach was in their area. We covered: Watts; Gardena; Compton; Lakewood; Central Long Beach; Torrance; several college campuses; and Down town LA.

We also make many contacts with local churches. Christ's Second Baptist in Long Beach pastored by Rev H. Gore became our home church. We met and developed many life long friendships within that church. Later, a group of prayer partners from within the church became our most faithful supporters. We did not receive support from the church directly, but people within the church.

We received very little support from churches themselves. One church sent a gift at Christmas; Another, sent at Easter; and three sent on a regular basis.

We would give an exceptional thanks to Unity Baptist and Greater Love Baptist of Los Angeles, and United Holy Church of Santa Ana, who are still standing with us today. Mostly, we are supported by individuals who send their gifts though our California office. In Japan, we lived off less than $400 per month, but things were cheaper then and we purchased food from the local farmers.

*Today we are looking for donors who will give towards schools, water wells, and church buildings and support National Pastors in Africa. When you see those who have nothing, then your little seems great!*

# Chapter 21

## Appointed school Dean for six months

After three months in the refresher course, the Dean, Frank Eiklor, requested a short break to go on a European tour with a team to Switzerland., Grace Brackett; Evelyn Tedford; and Martha Ingram. Bro Shelley approached me regarding taking his place for the next term. This suited us well for it gave us housing and food while we deputated in the area.

Having taught in Japan and led the Fisherman's club, the classes in Long Beach were easier. I did not need a translator. However, one very important thing that happened, A Japanese leader in Kyoto wrote me regarding sending his son to be in my classes. Not knowing anything about him, we invited him to come.

Masaru was an outstanding student. He excelled in his studies and was eager to learn how to evangelize his own community. We used his testimony on the radio and I took him to Gardena and Torrance to evangelize the local Japanese community at that time.

Today Masaru is the head of a large Japanese Judeo-Christian movement in Japan. They have a tremendous impact on the local region from Kyoto to Tokyo. They also have a special relationship with Israel and send students to the Hebrew University in Tele Aviv. Many speak Hebrew and witness to "God's Chosen" people. It is just so beautiful to see what God has done among them.

## A New Directive

As our furlough time was nearing its end, we began praying earnestly for a clear direction from God regarding our next field of service. The Quisenberrys had moved on to South America and the plans for Okinawa changed. We did not feel the call to return to Okinawa.

We prayed about several countries. Bro Lee spoke fondly of London England, but we had felt a tug in our hearts for Africa. We had read much of the great needs in West Africa since most White missionaries at that time were calling that region a missionary graveyard. Few wanted to go to West, Africa, so it was most needy, and we felt God would have us go there. We researched the countries of the area, discovered that Nigeria was very progressive, and had many educated people along with a large University in Ibadan.

We appeared before the board with charts and reports on the most populous African Nation in the world and presented the needs with the majority being non-Christian; Muslims; Animists; and Jujisuists, and other tribal rituals. We appealed for a transfer from Japan and the Orient to Nigeria, West Africa, and the Board granted the transfer. For the next six months, we raised funds for our new field of service, Nigeria, Africa.

When we came on furlough after each four-year term, two of our own family members always welcomed us. Being a growing family of six, they never said we could not have you here.

The first family was James and Odessa Taylor of Los Angeles, my brother and sister-in-law. James, the seventh child, was twenty years my senior and treated me as a son. They welcomed us and looked after us every time. We dared to come to LA and stay in a hotel when he had a large home so near.

Odessa was the best cook Alabama produced. She would cook special dishes for the children and a melt-in- your –mouth lemon cake. Hospitality was their gift, and because of them, we stayed in California to do most of our fund raising. If we had paid rent for the short-time stays, we would not have been able to return to the field so soon.

The second family was Dorothy's first cousin, Martha, and John Alley and their five children. Martha was an evangelist and had taught Dorothy in Sunday school in Waco. Once we were visiting and staying in Long Beach, and there was a small charge for our room and board. Martha asked us to move to her home, in order to accumulate funds for our return trip to the field. She called Dorothy her "little sister," and they treated her as if she was.

Elgin, age 3 with
Parents in Texas
cotton field

Elgin
as a
Marine
1956

Mission Headquarters

Kishiba, Nikagusuku Mission -1960

New
Arrivals
on the
Island.

Japan Ministry

University Fisherman's Club

Quisenberry Family 1960, Who
inspired us for Missions

Film Ministry

Children's
Service
before
Village
Film
Ministry

Japan Ministry 1960

Some of
the
Children
in
Dorothy's
Youth
Ministry

Special
Celebrations
with the
Japanese
Senior
Church
Members

Idol Burning

Kuniyoshi Family, 1960

Pastor Shinyu, Papa
Kuniyoshi and Neighbor.

Students visiting our home on a holiday outing

Okinawa Christian School, Classes 5-8, 1961

David Feng being tutored in ESL class, 1962

Koza Four Corners Ministry 1961 - 1963

Our Family in Japan, 1962

David Feng , ® with wife and son, is now an executive with Ford
Motor Co.

Return in 1999

Elgin Teaching in Nakagusuku
Church

Dorothy holding child, with Obaason
Kunioshi, 94, Mitsuko Arkaki and a
Daughter of the house.

# Part Three
## Chapter 22

### Off to West Africa!

Amid lots of tears and farewells, the headquarters staff, along with several friends and family members bid us goodbye at the Union Pacific Railroad station in Los Angeles. We were to travel across country by train via; Texas; Illinois; Detroit; and New York to say goodbye to our family for another four years.

During the trip, we were reminded again, America is still not a friendly place for Afro-Americans. We had to take the last car, the last seats, and the noisiest spot on the train.

Having two small children, this was not pleasant. The conductor opened and closed the rear door beside us repeatedly to signal the driver when the tracks were clear. It was so disturbing that the children became fretful and being December, it was very cold.

We bid farewell to our family in Dallas and Waco, then on to Dorothy's elder sister, Zeila and Aunt, Martha, who were in Chicago at that time; then to Detroit to visit my three older sisters and two older brothers, and their families. Again, we contacted the Nigerian embassy to see if our visas were there, for they had not arrived before leaving California. The Embassy officials said they had no records of them, so we would have to re-apply, which we did. However, we would have to purchase our tickets for Africa immediately in order to get a discount fare for a family of four.

After a time of prayer, my wife and I decided to try applying at another Embassy in Africa and then try again for Nigeria later. As God would have it, we applied at the Liberian Embassy and got a visa immediately. We purchased airline tickets to Liberia from Detroit via Lisbon, Portugal. After spending a week in Detroit, we flew to Liberia.

Arriving in Liberia is a story all its own! When we disembarked, at 5pm, we discovered that the capital city, Monrovia was 20 miles from the airport, and we must a hire a taxi for $25. After bartering with the Taxi drivers, the price was standard, so we took a cab. About twelve miles out, our taxi spurted and stopped in the middle of the bush country (jungle to you). The driver walked around the car a few times, checked under the hood, and then looked sheepishly at us and said, "The car is out of gas. I will flag a ride, pick up a can of petrol, and soon come. Stay in the car, for dark will soon come, all the animals come at night."

We were not sure what else to do or if he would return, but did stay in the car. Lo, and behold, the animals came, jumping all over the car, some peering into or banging on the windows. It was at dusk and they could see us; Monkeys; baboons; and several wild cats all came and jumped on the car. We felt like we were in a zoo but just the opposite was true, we were in a cage and the animals were watching us.

Elgin Jr (4) said, "Mommy, I don't think we are going to like Africa." I am scared of the dark and all these animals! We reassured him that it would not always be as this once we were in town.

The driver returned in what seemed like an eternity, but was only about 30 minutes. He put the petrol in and took us to a hotel in Monrovia, where we spent the night. The next morning we contacted a missionary friend in the area named, Maggie Lampkins, who ran a local orphanage and another group from Atlanta, Carver Missions.

Maggie warmly welcomed us and gave us a tour of the facility, afterwards she had her driver take us to visit with Henrietta Mears and a two other Afro American Missionaries, out of Atlanta, GA. Henrietta was house sitting and child minding the children of Howard O. Jones. Howard and wife worked with the Billy Graham Crusades for many years. They were in Liberia with a radio ministry at ELWA (Eternal Love Winning Africa) we were invited to stay on the Compound in Howard's home since he and his wife were in Canada.

*This was our introduction to Africa!* The next week was spent sharing our testimonies over the air at the Radio station; and visiting the Nigerian Embassy to secure a visa. Early the next week we received, word that our visas were granted! The missionaries all rejoiced with us, even though they made it clear that we could stay in Liberia and work with ELWA since we had much experience in radio broadcasting.

As soon as we could purchase tickets, we flew to Lagos, with a stop over in Ghana. This was the Days when the First President, Nkrumah was in power and the Red Chinese under Mao Satang served as bodyguards for Nkrumah. We did not leave the airport in Accra, due to the armed Chinese militia everywhere However, We prayed for Ghana that God would keep his hand over her.

In Lagos, we stayed at the SIM guesthouse on Elizabeth Road. It was clean, air conditioned and quiet for the children. Dorothy and I would take turns going to church services, as Willis was still asthmatic and we did not want to expose him to much dust and diesel fumes from the mama wagons on the streets. They were called Mama Wagons for it was mostly the women with their children on their backs who did the trading and selling. We were just a few blocks from the bridge that crossed over into Lagos proper, so we could watch the people selling and bartering for goods all day long. This was our first introduction to street markets so it was interesting to see how they finally sold something.

The missionaries in charge of the guesthouse were very particular about the meals. If you were not going to make it back in time for lunch or the 5pm supper, you must let them know before leaving. This was a tricky issue, for being new to the area; we were not sure how long it would take to travel around town. Due to the lunch being the main meal, we would come back for lunch, and then go out again in the afternoon. Many days I would say do not expect us, as we do not know how long we will be, seeing that we were house hunting.

After a week, we located a small two-bedroom duplex owned by British American Tobacco Co. It was fully furnished, even down to an inventory of cutlery, dishes, linens, and small appliances. There was also a small one room empty shack in the rear. When we inquired, we were told that it was for our houseboy. It did not look nice enough for a dog.

Immediately, we were approached by many people regarding why we were here. One Hausa businessman, a devout Muslim, came by each day on his way home. He asked questions about Afro-Americans, such as, "Why so few of us came to Africa as missionaries?" I could only say that my people were struggling for their civil rights in the US. Therefore, they were fearful of rejection. They did not want to come to a foreign country and not be welcomed. Moreover, they were not welcomed by the various mission agencies.

By this time, I had done some research and learned that Black Missionaries had gone out after the civil War, but they had been mistreated and ill handled by White Overseers. Later the Caucasian missionaries asked that no blacks be sent to their area to work. Therefore, Jim Crow was also on the mission fields around the world. Gradually, the doors closed in missions, just as it did in the schools, the colleges, and the churches of America.

Within a few days of being in Lagos, we started a twice-weekly Bible study with eight young men. Four were Ibos from the Eastern Region; two were Hausas from the North; and two were Yoruba of the Western Region. Gradually, all but one made a decision for Christ. Strangely enough, it was one from Port Harcourt, a Catholic area who did not receive the gift of eternal life. He felt that each time he took communion he received Christ. We faithfully continued to teach the Book of Saint John, then Romans and lastly the Book of Ephesians.

We were still trying to get a permanent visa, since we were only given a tourist one. Several mission agencies offered to become our sponsors. Sudan Interior Mission (SIM) especially invited us to work with them in Jos for Dorothy could teach in their school and I could work with the ministries they had there. However, we did not feel led to accept their offers and decided we would remain with our present organization.

In our second week, our Hausa friend asked if his daughter could come and work for us. We had not thought we needed a worker, for the work was not hard since we used the bathtub for washing. We soon learned that you had to carry the large tubs for washing and the buckets of water from the street taps. We were to use the house taps for drinking and bath water only.

That weekend, we decided to have the daughter, Felicity, come, and see how she got on. At first, she insisted on sleeping in the little shack out back, because everyone said that was where she had to sleep. After two nights Dorothy asked her how was she doing? Oh, she said, I cannot sleep out there, it's scary all locked in with no light or fresh air, and the mosquitoes are bad! How do those guys do it?

Dorothy approached me regarding letting her sleep on the living room floor. She already had a rolled mat out in the little shack. We offered her the living room floor. Immediately we saw a difference in the girl. Her eyes glowed, as she became more open towards us; she also became our daughter and friend instead of just our maid, helping with ideas and local shopping tips.

Some of the neighbors whispered that we should not let "them" stay in the house, for "they" would steal everything or let someone else in to do it. This was a young schoolgirl about fourteen, who was afraid to be alone in an isolated shack outside. If she had been our daughter, we would not have wanted her living in those circumstances.

Her parents seemed delighted that we wanted to treat her as a daughter instead of a maid, so they sent us a special gift of a carved elephant lamp. Later they also refused extra money to pay for her helping us pack and carry suitcases for our trip.

At the end of our fifth week, the then Prime Minister, Mr. Boliwaa, a Hausa was assassinated. Word began to spread, that an Ibo had killed him. At our next Bible Study, all four Ibo men were absent, but nothing was said to us. When they were also absent at the next meeting I made a remark about it, and prayed for them.

As I said before, Felicity had become our friend and accepted the Lord. She was more than a servant to us; she began to explain to Dorothy in the kitchen what was happening to the Ibos. In the meantime, I had gone to call on Victor and Steven, two of the most interested Ibo men. As I knocked at their door, a lady came up and said "No one is there; they are all fleeing back to the East. People are threatening to kill all the Ibo s due to the killing of the Prime Minister. Things are heating up around here."

By this time, Felicity had also told my wife of the problems. She also said, my Dad thinks you should leave before a war breaks out. The papers are saying that a civil war is coming between the Hausa in the North and the Ibos in the East. Because the Ibos were Catholic and had the oil in their region, they wanted to separate from the rest of the country and keep the oil for themselves. They want to call their separate country, *Biafra*.

This situation grew and became *The Biafra Crisis; Nigeria's civil war from 1965–1969*. Naturally, I wanted to keep my family safe, so I went into town and bought two papers along with a small radio so I could listen to the BBC and VOA (Voice of America).

The news was frightening; all foreigners were asked to prepare to leave Nigeria ASAP on the VOA. The BBC was saying go to the nearest safe country. We had not received any funds from our Long Beach office for they had only just learned that we had made it to Nigeria. However, we had received the money for the sale of our house in Okinawa a few weeks before we left for Africa, and it was in our savings account.

We checked with several persons regarding the next two countries, and then called Togo and De Homey now called Togo and Cameroon. They were French speaking and we did not want to begin learning another language. London seemed to be the best place. Most all the highest achieving African students were sent there to study. God also gave us a word from Isaiah 25: 6-7 *"In this mountain (place, London), God will make a feast of fat things...and he will destroy the face covering cast over all people and the Vail which is spread over all nations..* We believed that God was saying that he would use us to help people from many nations come to the truth of the Gospel in London. They could be trained; and in turn carry the Gospel to their own people. This excited us, as we could see Africans who already knew the languages and culture returning to teach their own people.

Hearing a word from God, we now felt prepared to take another big a step. You should be aware also, that this was not easy. We had people praying for us as we flew to Africa for us to establish a ministry. We had been sure that God had called us to go there. Now we would have to explain to those same prayer partners and supporters as to how we could have gotten things so wrong, and that God was now sending us to Britain.

In the end, we could only say that God sent us to Africa for a short time and had allowed us to see the needs there, but he had not allowed us to remain. Just why we did not know nor did, we understand the reason why.

Immediately I went to BOAC to purchase tickets to London. They had their next flight out in two days at 5am, so we had to be ready at that time. Only BOAC and Pan Am were still flying so we had to be ready. The American planes were full and with no seats available. Doesn't this sound like Okinawa all over again? We begin to search our hearts and inquire from God. Why Lord, why Us? God just silently continued to remind us, He is in control, and why not, us. God gave us more scriptures and assurances that this is what He wanted for us.

# Part Four
## Chapter 23

## Arrival in London, England

On March 2, 1965, we arrived at London Heathrow airport, a family of four with three suitcases and $60us in our pocket. It had taken all our savings to purchase the tickets. The British Customs agent asked how long we planned to be in Britain. We didn't have a ready answer. "Who are you going to stay with or visit" "We had been sent the address of a friend of the mission, who invited us to work with him. The Customs agent said, "With a family of four and only $60, I shouldn't let you into the country, Mr. Taylor! But since I believe you are a missionary and an honest man, I'm going to give you three months and you can extend this later." Wow, we made it, by God's Grace and favor; then boarded a train to Victoria station.

We were so weary after traveling with a fifteen months old, and a four and half year old; that we flagged down a taxi and asked the driver to take us to an economical hotel for the night The Hotel was in nice Victorian style edifice. We had a large triple sized room with double bed and two small ones, along with a living room area. It was just around the corner from Victoria Station. They provided bed and breakfast but we were to go out for other meals.

When we awaken the next morning, the ground was covered with snow. Could you imagine, we had just left Africa and arrived in London with only thin summer clothes and shoes! However we did have the jackets we had traveled across the US in our cases, my wife had seen that we kept those even in Africa. After breakfast, which was served in the basement, I put on my coat and thin shoes and tackled the snow, walking to a red telephone booth, which were common at that time.

Pay phones in England were quite complicated. After three failed attempts, I dialed the operator and asked for the instructions. Being a stranger in the country, I didn't know the names of the small coins. She instructed me to put in a *thre p'ny bit and* push button A; after the tone, put in a *ta'-pence* and push button B. Not understanding her Cockney, I asked, "Which of the coins are those? She quirked, "Go ask someone who speaks English and hung up? Well now, what was I to do? I left the booth and asked two fellows nearby for the names of the coins in my hand, They were helpful as they smiled at my story and said it was usually common for the two penny to be called *ta'-pence* and the three penny was called *thre p'ny*. Well, there goes my knowledge of English. This was like a foreign country. Everyone from various section of the country spoke a different dialect, along with those from the entire British common wealth of nations.

Upon calling the family who invited us, I learned that they had taken in another missionary couple and their place was no longer available. Then I asked if they knew of another place we could stay, they didn't know of any except perhaps a hostel.

I returned to our room and told Dorothy the news and happenings of the day. Later I went out again and called an Irish couple who were to come and work with us in London. They were very disappointed with the English, finding them very reserved and distant; they were returning to Ireland. Nevertheless, they did give us the telephone number of a lady who housed missionaries in her home, Mrs. Edith Rush.

When I called Mrs. Rush, she sounded so nice over the phone. Of course, we could come; she had a studio flat on the top floor with a kitchenette that would be available for us the next morning at four Pounds a week. ($12) plus we put shillings in the electric and gas meters as we used them. What a relief, the Hotel was charging 9 pounds per night and we had to stay on for one more night for it was past checkout time.

At checkout time the next day, we flagged a taxi to take us to 108 Vassel Road in Brixton, SW9. Mrs. Rush and her daughter met us at the door and welcomed us with a hot cup of tea and scones (Biscuits in US). Cookies are called biscuits in Britain. They then took us to the top floor of the four-story house and showed us our room. It was a large room with four single beds, side by side; a small kitchenette with a sink and two burner stove top, and a sofa. There were two large bright windows looking out over Elephant and Castle, and downtown London. It also over looked two large gas works.

We were so relieved to have found something affordable so soon, that we were highly elated. Mrs. Rush shared with us that she had housed over fifteen hundred missionaries over the past thirty years and that God had blessed her with this as a ministry of love. She had been an abused wife and others had helped her. Now she wanted to help others in need of housing.

Remember that we had said that our funds had not reached us from the time we left Detroit! They still had not come. We called Long Beach and gave them the address of the local American Express Bank, for those were the arrangements we made with our office. They were to wire funds to the local American Express and we would pick it up with our Passports as ID.

For the next four and a half weeks, we did not hear from the office. Little did we know that they were waiting for the checks they had sent to Nigeria to return before writing another? Somehow, the newly appointed bookkeeper did not know that she could cancel those previously sent checks, and write new ones. She had only kept local books before, therefore she did not realize how long it would take for foreign ones to return, if ever

Remember we only had $60 US when we arrived, that was just about right to cover the two nights at a hotel and three weeks with Mrs. Rush. Again, God choose to feed us another way. At Mrs. Rush, we got bed and breakfast, oatmeal; tea; and toast each morning.

Our first Sunday, I visited a local Baptist church and sat next to a Jamaican gentleman, Rev. L. A. Rowe. Bro. Rowe as we later called him owned a Caribbean grocery store in Stock well Park. We talked about our arrival and what we felt God was leading us to do in England. He enquired as to our address, and said he would drop by to see us sometime.

The following day, Mrs. Rush announced that we had a caller. Since we didn't know anyone, we went down to see who it could be. It was Bro Rowe. He came up and talked all about his working in American many years before. Then he said, "I brought a few things for you out in the car. Thought I would check first and see if you could use them."

I went down stairs with him and he had two boxes of groceries for us. Isn't that like our God! He allowed a stranger to feel us without our even telling him that we had a need. The food lasted until the very day that our funds arrived at the bank.

Twice each week I caught a double-decked red bus and went to the bank to check on our funds. Returning one afternoon when I had received no news, I was praying silently on the top deck when I looked up and saw a large sign which said, *"Take Courage"*

Being a new arrival, I hadn't seen that sign before; I quietly thought, "That is just what I need. I'm going to go find that church and speak to the pastor. Alighting from the bus, I made my way to the "church" and opened the door, to my amazement; it was a Pub (an English Bar). As I shared this experience with Mrs. Rush, she smiled and said, "Elgin those signs are all over Britain, for *"Courage"* is a local beer!"

I can say to this day that sign encouraged me and I will never forget the experience. Dorothy was keeping a diary during this time and when you read the notes; you will find a notation, NT, not today-over and over again, for over four weeks. On April 6, she wrote, "Today we spent our last pound on milk for the children. Lord we need to hear from you. We know the funds are coming but we need them, today. That afternoon, the funds arrived at the bank and I was able to come home with awesome news. There was much rejoicing in the Taylor household that evening. In fact, we went to a little hamburger place called Wimpy's around the corner and celebrated.

We were able to hunt for an apartment so that we could move into our own place. England at this time had signs against renting to the Irish and coloreds, however, their coloreds was much broader than in the USA. They included Orientals, Indians, and Caribbean people.

We signed up with a large housing agency that had a fair rent policy in place and promised they would have an apartment for us within in two weeks. They sent us to three areas and finally we located a very nice large two-bedroom place in Wandsworth, on Burntwood Court Road. By the weekend, we were able to move in and have separate bedrooms for the children, two months after arriving in London. We had lived in a one-room studio flat in single beds side by side for over eight weeks; with a two-burner hot plate for a stove; and no refrigerator. Perishables were sat outside on the windowsill until needed. Milk was delivered every morning and we went out for fresh veggies daily.

We were finally going to be an ordinary family again! Praise God for his manifold blessings bestowed upon us. We didn't see any of this as extra ordinary, but now looking back, we realize how must God worked over time to get us where he wanted us to be, in spite of our pushing against closed doors to force them open.

I sum it up by saying like the Apostle Paul: I Cor 13:12; NKJ: "For now we see through a glass, darkly, but then face to face; now I know in part, but; but then I shall know as even also I am known."

We entered England with great expectancy and sought out those churches and people with whom he wanted us to work.

# Chapter 24

## Training Program Opens at Brixton Baptist Church

Our first weekend in London found us visiting Brixton Baptist Church near the Brixton Market area of South London. We had noted the service times upon passing it while shopping.

Within three weeks of arriving in England, we were regular attendees of Brixton Baptist Church, where the Pastor, Rev. James encouraged us to share our vision of outreach with the congregation. He expressed the need for more evangelism among the many immigrants, especially, in the Brixton Market. This was a large open street market where people of all nationalities came for international foods. It was "the real in place to shop" in South London in the 1960s. Here you could find almost any foreign food or foreign produced product you desired. We found many Afro-American hair products, Jet and Ebony magazines, yams, black-eyed peas, and other soul foods there.

Rev. James continued to encourage us to start an outreach ministry in his area. Several of his members invited us to their homes for tea the following week, and we were welcomed by many of the English, as well as the many Caribbean believers.

One couple, from Jamaica, had us over the following Tuesday at half past five. We were expecting a nice evening meal, so didn't feed the boys so as not to spoil their dinner. However, we soon learned that a British Tea meant small bits and pieces such as opened face sandwiches, coffee, cake, tea, and other snacks. Young Elgin, age five, kept asking for more food, as the snacks was very light, so his mother gently told him, "we must make due with what we were given for now, and when we returned home I would fix him something special, like spaghetti." After this learning experience, we always knew that if someone invited us for high tea around five or sixpm; it would be just a snack.

Another couple from Jamaica invited us to Sunday Dinner, Rupert and Anita Johnson. They put on a feast of curry goat, achee with salt fish, rice and peas, baked swordfish, curry chicken, and rum fruitcake with pudding. The main drink was strained carrot juice. This was our second introduction to Caribbean foods, and we really appreciated it.

Three senior English ladies had us over quite regularly, sometimes just for a cup of tea and other times for a lamb or beef dinner. They also became our first donors in England, as they supported our ministry on a quarterly basis.

In June of 1965, we began a Bible study and Tuesday "Action Night" at the home of Anita and Rupert Johnson and their two daughters, Joy (8) and Vivien (6). Anita shared how she had agonized in prayer, going into the restrooms at work, pleading for God to send some one to help reach the many nationalities in Brixton for Jesus. She went on to say, "I know God sent you as an answer to my prayers." Her home was like a grand central station most of the time, as she had the most wonderful gift of hospitality and helps that we have ever encountered.

Later we learned that Anita was dyslexic, and so were many other women from the Caribbean Islands. Some were dyslexic through a lack of opportunity to attend school, for in most rural areas, farmers sent sons to school, not daughters. Several were real dyslexics, and saw things back to front.

Others, who joined with us during this time, were Rev. L. A. Rowe, a local minister and businessman. New converts: Bro. and Sister Green; Millie McPherson; and Sis Gladys Monroe; Bro. Gordon; Freddie and Ida Brown; and Rupert and Anita Johnson served on the board of Christians in Action UK for many years.

During this time, Rev. Rowe introduced us to many local Caribbean pastors. Each Saturday afternoon we drove to meetings and conferences all around the Southern UK. Being a newcomer, they invited me to speak repeatedly. Two Pastors from the New Testament Church, Pastor Powell and Pastor Bernard, became our close friends. They invited us to run evangelism outreach in their church. Over the years, they have always welcomed us when we are in London. Sadly, I had to refuse invitations as our growing family needed more attention on weekends and the college was making more demands of our time.

We signed an agreement to lease a property in Stockton through a local lawyer in charge of the estate. An elderly church member, in a nursing home, owned the property. The trustees of her estate had arranged the lease documents and given us the keys to begin cleaning up the house, which had been empty for two years. We allowed two of our first students to move in while cleaning and re-decorating.

Two relatives of the property owner protested having anyone move into the house while she was still living, as they felt it would hasten her death and be a bad omen. Unbeknown to the relatives, we had already signed the agreement, and our students had moved into the house. However, being Christians and not wanting to begin our ministry on a negative note, we agreed to tear up the lease and start afresh seeking another property.

This was an enormous set back for us, for now there was nowhere to house the students in training. We scrambled to locate another place. We accommodated the two male students by renting a large studio flat for them in a local home. As time passed and no other building was immediately available, Pastor James stepped in and offered us the use of the Brixton Baptist Church Hall and other church facilities for our classes

In the hall, we held daily classes; served lunch; and sent out evangelism teams. Pastor James also taught once per week along side Caroline Rotz, and myself, while Dorothy, prepared the evening meals for the staff and students. This was Dorothy's way of contributing to the ministry, while also managing to stay home with our two sons.

Our first students were quite multi-cultural, a Jamaican, Sister Inez Gordon; an Irishman, Billy Patterson; and an Englishman, Tony Lacey. They were very dedicated and committed. They had a full daily schedule, classes in the mornings; house to house witnessing three afternoons per week; then market or street meets the last two afternoons. The course at that time was six months in length.

After the fifth and tenth weeks, the students were given specially planned, *"sealed orders"*; on such occasion, they were to arrive well dressed and prepared to fulfill the instructions in their sealed envelops. These sessions were designed to build faith and confidence. Faith ministries in the 50s through 70s used this method to train student. It was to help visualize, "That they can do all things through Christ." It also added interest, flavor, and excitement to the courses.

Even though this was many years ago, I can recall, as if it were today, sending the two men to the newly built post office tower and the Nigerian embassy. The two ladies, Caroline collaborated with Inez, were sent to the American Express Bank and Trafalgar Square. Each team returned with glowing reports of open doors and being able to witness to many persons in authority.

The last assignment given was "The faith Trek." Just as Christ sent out the seventy-two in Luke 10: two by two and instructed them not to take money or food for their journey, we would take or send the students to a nearby town without any food or little or no money. (A staff member went with the women and they would take money for bus fares and telephone, for safety) They were to trust God to supply food and transportation back to Brixton, the ladies by evening and the men by the next morning. This was always a blessed time. It renewed the students' confidence in God, themselves, and their fellowman. Often, people would assist them and offer British tea without knowing their circumstances. The students shared upon their return that they had only stated as much as they had been instructed, "We are Bible School students studying to go to a mission field and calling in your neighbor hood. Many times someone would invite them in, give them tea, and also give them a small monetary gift.

God blessed this class; they completed the missionary training college, and became home missionaries. The two men became pastors and Inez, who is now deceased, became immersed in youth work, first at our church and later in another local church.

In the meantime, Christians in Action Missions had planted many workers in Europe. It was decided through the missionaries and from our Headquarters that they should all come to London for a conference. At the 1966 conference in London, I was elected Director for Europe. The following year CinA held its 10 - year anniversary.

During this time, CinA held a special 10-Year Anniversary in California. As the European Directed, I was required to attend. We flew home to the conference and joined four other Field and Area Directors for planning "New Horizons" for the ministry.

Having the larger field at that time, we reported on the five –year plans we already had in place for Europe. Many of the missionary delegates were excited by the plans for expanding and team building focus.

I stayed in the US for two months before returning to London. This time was spent on support building. Our ministry was growing and so was our family.

God opened a special door of opportunity for me at McDougal-Douglas Aircraft Co. A group of Christian men held a weekly prayer service in the plant. They invited me to share on my ministry with the group.

Looking back, it was a God ordained time. Six men and their families took us on as their missionaries and supported us for many years. Harold and Lois McDaniel headed that group and they faithfully collected the pledges each month and sent them in to the office. They will never know how much that helped us as a family and the ministry in London. Brethren, Thank you for being there. We esteem you highly in the Lord.

# Chapter 25

# A Third Son, Timothy Paul, joins Our Family

While preparing for all the Missionaries to come to London, we were also preparing for the arrival of a new family member. This also meant that Dorothy would not be able to carry the full load of the cooking as she had in the past. One of the missionaries traveling to Italy, Virginia Straughn came to spend time with us. While there, she agreed to take over the kitchen duties in Dorothy's place. This was a blessing for our family life. Dorothy was able to spend more time with the boys and preparing for the addition...

During the Christmas Holidays, 1965, we held the first European Regional conference in London at Brixton Baptist Church. Fifteen delegates attended: From Spain; Dale and Janet Simpson, and Shirley Cash; Germany: Martha Fritz and Grace Brackett; Switzerland: Martha Ingram, Gerald Houston, and Evelyn Tedford; Italy; Tom and Irene Hodges; Ireland Anna Todd and Mary Smyth; and from England: Caroline Rotz, Virginia Straughn, and Dorothy and myself. The conference elected me to serve as Regional Director for Europe, a post that I held for seventeen years, until being elected International President in 1982.

Eight months after opening the training college, the Taylor family celebrated the arrival of Timothy Paul, who announced his arrived March 28, 1966, very early in the morning. His two elder brothers were delighted for a baby. However, elder brother, Elgin Jr. (6) did not understand why we could not just choose one of the pretty pink baskets out of the hospital nursery window. "We already have two blue ones (boys)," he said, "So now we need a pink one (girl)." After a chat with his father, he accepted that the blue one was our very own and was pleased as punch to be mom's helper in taking him home

Timothy was the ideal baby, quiet, non-fussy, and a well beloved addition to the family. His mother was able to devote more time to the home, as she was temporary relieved of cooking by Virginia Straughn, a missionary appointee to Italy. Later, Dorothy continued to cook for the school and assist where needed. She is a devoted wife and most committed mother, but she is also richly blessed with the gift of helps, discernment, and encouragement. You may note, throughout this book, that there is a positive attitude, which has always emulated from her, even in our most troubled and testing times.

Again, you will observe on many occasions, when a word of knowledge was needed, she was always there with suggestions and ideas. I have to admit, I did not always appreciate her gifts as much as I should have, but down through the years, I grew to depend on her abilities more and more. Not many wives would travel to so many countries (about 85, for her and 94 for me; under poor housing conditions; many times on very rough, hot, and dusty roads, with very poor and non-air conditioned transportation; But she has never complained about those conditions, just endured them and accepted them.

This is a small tribute to her for her dedication to our family, our ministry, and me for over forty-seven years at this writing. She would fill a void in the ministry, wherever needed whether cook; cleaner; bookkeeper; Prayer letter writer; and finally, newspaper editor, a position she held for the ten years before retiring. Therefore, I would say, Thank you, Dorothy for standing beside me all these years.

Rev. John McNickols of Hayden's Park Baptist Church in Wimbledon, England dedicated Timothy on Easter Sunday, 1966. Pastor McNickols was also the Chief Editor of *"The Sunday Companion"* magazine which was enclosed with the *London Times* on Weekends. He immediately published an article on our ministry in the paper, which opened the door for many new contacts and inquiries.

# Chapter 26

## Bible Study and Multi-Cultural Outreach in Brixton

The Brixton Market area of London during the 1960s through the 1980s the most multicultural place in Britain. If there was a food needed from almost anywhere in the world available, you could usually find it in Brixton. We began a Bible study and outreach at the Johnson's flat twice weekly. Tuesdays we had a group Bible study and went out witnessing door to door for one hour before. On Thursdays, those with new converts would gather and go out to call on them. This was called "Follow-up."

The ministry and church grew because of this outreach. At first, we invited the new believers to Brixton Baptist Church. However, due to it being very conservative and reserved in its worship, the multiculturalism was not fitting in to well. The newly arrived immigrants desired more jubilance in expression plus more variations in the music. It seems that all around the world music and singing is a great drawing card for the church.

There were over a hundred young people who came to Christ in this outreach and several hundred adults. Many only attended the Wednesday night Bible study, so we had to seek for a larger place. Families were beginning to attend a Bible study in someone's home. There were people standing in the hallway many weeks, so we began to pray for a larger meeting place.

The next "Giant Step" in the ministry was to find a permanent building to house the school. After much prayer, we were lead by Pastor McNickols to contact Miss Evelyn Elphick in South Norwood. She was in the process of closing down a private grammar school, which he suggested, might be the ideal place for a small boarding school. Upon seeing the building, a large Victorian house on four floors next to Norwood Lake, we loved it! Just one small problem, we were faith missionaries with no set income, how could we commit to a lease or long term contract.

After much prayer and fasting, the three of us, Dorothy, Caroline and I, called on Evelyn and shared the vision God had given us for using the building as a Missionary training and commissioning center. Evelyn became very animated and excited. "Oh," She said, "I would love to have a group like you living here. Could you move in at month's end and pay L20 British Pounds (approx. $60 US) per week?" ($3US equaled to L1 British Pounds in 1966). "Then, she continued, the floors wouldn't be empty." She occupied a one bedroom flat on the fourth floor, and there were two extra large rooms left on that floor.

Evelyn went on to say, "If you could sign an annual agreement, then all I would require is for you to pay the agents fees for drafting the agreement, and two weeks rent in advance." This amounted to about L150 British Pounds ($450 US). The utilities were extremely high, costing approximately L50monthly ($150). Well that seemed a bit steep for only the lights and gas, for we still had to purchase coal for the heating system. The building was large with ten-foot ceilings, which would give us another huddle to cross in the winter. We departed, stating we would give her a decision at the beginning of the week.

# Chapter 27

## Full-Time CinA Bible College Established

My wife and I had prayed and gone over our total projected income, very carefully. Then she made a suggestion, that we take responsibility for the rent ourselves; our income was low but it would cover the rent, and a few other expenses, thereby clearing the way for a contractual agreement to be signed. Caroline's small income would cover most of the electric bill; set the income from the students to cover their food and the heating bills; thereby meeting our full budget. After sharing this plan with Caroline, we all agreed that by faith, we would take this step and sign the agreement for two years. Needless to say, we were able to pay the deposit by month's end and moved in within ten days.

In July 1966, we moved to 36 Lancaster Road, South Norwood, where by August; the excitement had swelled to fever pitch. We frantically re-decorated all three floors for staff and students. The Taylor family occupied the middle floor, with Auntie Caroline, Evelyn Elphick, and the women students on the top floor; and the first/ground floor housed the men; two offices; along with the large assembly room; which would be the main classroom and chapel, and also used for services on Sundays.

By the way, we discovered that the basement was occupied by a missionary family on furlough, who wanted to stay until the end of the year. This was another unseen work of God, for that family paid us six pounds per week to remain downstairs, so this left us to pay only fourteen pounds weekly until the end of the year

When the full-time student body arrived, it was a cross-cultural group, a mature man, David Hall, who had been a British American Tobacco Co executive in East Africa: A youth out of high school, Bill Bud, and Margaret Mair, an English woman from the midlands. Some of our own Bible study group enrolled for the day classes only, Sister Anita Johnson; and Ida Williams (Brown) among them.

During this time, we soon learned that Anita was dyslexic, and so were many other women from the Caribbean Islands. Some were dyslexic through a lack of opportunity to attend school, for in most rural areas, if farmers sent anyone to classes; it was sons, not daughters. Several were truly classed as dyslexics, seeing things in a back to front way.

Dorothy volunteered to teach an English class (ESL) for several illiterate persons. Anita was an aggressive student, and so was a woman from Italy, Lily Comanci. They were motivated to read. They both really desired with all their hearts, to read the Bible. When Dorothy noticed that Anita had committed a great number of hymns to memory, she devised a strategy of having her follow the words in the hymnal as she sang in order to build a vocabulary and develop her word recognition. After some research, at Scripture Union Book Stores, we also obtained information pertaining to a special Bible, with only a 1200 word vocabulary, which was printed especially for dyslexic or ESL (English as a Second Language) students. We ordered six copies and used them in our specially arranged Bible studies for the women.

As for myself, I was busy teaching daily, counseling staff and missionaries and making new contacts with many local pastors. One, Pastor Moffat, volunteered his time to come and teach once a week and joined our board of directors. Many weekends were spent building a relationship among the numerous West Indian Pastors. At first, I preached at special gatherings from London to Bedford, but it was always at my own expense, for all the immigrants were just beginning ministries across the British Isles. Later, due to the growing ministry and needs of your own family, I had to withdraw from those services except the occasional special celebration of very close friends.

Tuesday Evenings were inspiring and exciting to me, as many youth came to join me in our "Action Nights" in Brixton. This was an amazing house-to-house outreach and we met so many people from all over the world. I was learning also, for it was soon pointedly shown to me, to use the term Caribbean with people from the Islands, in the place of, Jamaican, as many of the new immigrants were from Barbados; Guyana; The Virgin Islands; Trinidad; and other places.

There were also Greeks, Eastern Europeans; Africans; and many others behind those doors. Gradually as the new converts grew, we realized the need for a building to assemble them on Sundays. There were few churches that welcomed foreigners openly, and the local services were reserved and quiet; not exuberant as the immigrants desired.

Having a goal to train and send Christians from various countries back to evangelize in their own country, made this new multi-cultural evangelism and discipleship program in the region more exciting. We felt it would be the catalyst for our training school in the future.

# Chapter 28

## Sunday school Program Established in Brixton

God answered our prayers for the children. We were able to rent a hall in downtown Brixton across from the Police station, for an afternoon Sunday school. Mrs. Johnson was the catalyst for getting this children's ministry underway. She and a team of women volunteered to go an hour before and cleanup and setup the chairs each Sunday in order for us to use this building.

The City Council agreed for its usage, but was not willing to clean it for us. Children were picked up by two or three vans each Sunday. Several church members along with our full-time missionaries became the teachers. We purchased flannel graph supplies from Scripture Union; ordered books from the USA; and purchased a speaker system.

The Police department was delighted to see an outreach to the youth of Brixton and they encouraged us as much as possible. They would let us know that they were keeping any older youth away that they thought were would be troublemakers.

Soon we had more children than we could safely handle in the building, so we had to seek for something different for the older youth. The church decided to rent another place on Friday evenings for the teens. We found a place very near many of our members in Stock well Estates. We could use the hall for a small payment and have a game night and devotionals for the youth. It was again setup similar to the Koza Fellowship center.

The teens would come and play various games, then after one hour, they would sit down for refreshments while a short testimony and devotional was presented. Those who showed interest in knowing more were taken to a quiet corner for follow up.

The parents became more involved when they saw the great results from the Fridays Youth Center. Many volunteered to cook cookies; prepare the hall; provide more chairs; and donate equipment. This program continued for three years. However, we never saw it take off at the church as it had in Brixton.

The Sunday school continued until 1980 when the Johnson family moved to New York. God greatly blessed the efforts and today we see many young adults who came to Christ though that ministry.

# Chapter 29

## Greater Steps Required! Purchasing our own Property!

After a year of Bible studies and outreach from the Johnson's flat (Apt) in Brixton, we began seeking a larger place. The school property was in a different area, and was several miles away, therefore we sought land, or buildings in the Brixton area, but none were located. The school property contained a small chapel from which the church leaders decided we should start holding a Sunday service. The many new converts and contacts of the outreach ministry began attending regularly.

Two of our first teenagers were Freddie Brown and Ida Williams, who later married, and taught Sunday school in Brixton. Freddie, also led the monthly men's fellowship for several years, and many of his brothers and sisters attended on special occasions.

The Johnson's daughters, Joy and Vivien, grew up in the ministry. They were part of the youth ministry, along with our sons, Elgin II, Willis, and Timothy. Michael, aged eight when we left England, was apart of our Sunday school program and enjoyed learning Bible verses and singing.

Willis and Tom Hodges Jr. were great friends. They contributed their musical and dramatic talents to all the youth activities at the church. Today, we are so pleased to see that they are yet exercising those talents while blessing their local churches. Willis has been a great asset to our ministry. He has been to Ghana with us twice and ran youth concerts and provided special music for the services.

Many, many, other youth grew up in the church some of note were the two Christie girls, the Brown sons; the Monroe children; the Chamber's sons; the Green family; 'the Montague family; Tom and Debbie Hodges; the Morris' sons; the Channers; and the McPherson family; and others. If I missed a name, I apologize; it just did not come to mind at this writing. God blessed our young people, and many are still serving God today! Richard and Sharon (Channer) McPherson are now pastoring in the Brixton Area.

# Chapter 30

## Our First British Church-Clyde Hall

Two of the first converts in South Norwood were an East Indian Hindu wife and mother, Patricia Martin, whom Dorothy had led to Christ one Action Night, and her husband, Marvin, whom I led to Christ while accompanying Dorothy on follow-up visits. Marvin showed a keen interest, but had many questions and misconceptions regarding, "Those Christians." Each week, they had many obstacles to overcome, but gradually they became more and more convinced of the claims of Christ. Becoming the only Christians in their respective families caused some separation from family gatherings, especially during Hindu holidays. They were hungry for the word, and grew rapidly in their spiritual walk; becoming the first ones baptized at the Lancaster Road location; and remained strong faithful members of the church, until 1970. They were relocated by the local council to a new housing development in Milton Keyes, Bedfordshire. This was our lost but the gain of another missionary couple, to whose church, we recommended the Martin family of five. We recently saw them at our fortieth anniversary celebrations in London. The children have grown up and they are still faithfully attending the fellowship in Bedford.

Soon the small chapel could no longer hold all the people. By the summer off 1967, we had leased a church hall on Clyde road in Addiscombe, which had the name "Clyde Hall" embossed in stone over the entrance. Here, the church grew rapidly. Many of the members of the church at that time developed fond memories of being baptized in the Clyde Hall baptistery, or dedicating their children there.

Our two Elder sons were part of the youth group and Dorothy taught the middle school children. Several missionaries joined us and taught various groups over the next three years.

# Chapter 31

## Lord and Lady Cyril Black dedicate our new Facility.

We leased both the Clyde Road and Lancaster Road properties, when the leases came up for renewal the Board suggested that we seek other properties. Being a great believer of investing in property and not wasting money on rent, I made a proposal to purchase a property for the college and for weekly church activities. This would not reduce our overhead expenses, but at least we would be gaining some investments of our own.

God gave us the Scriptural promises of Isaiah 54:2-4, "Enlarge the place of thy tent; and let them stretch forth the curtains of thine habitations: spare not; lengthen thy cords; and strengthen thy stakes."

We held a fundraiser at South Norwood Halls and many faith promises came in to cover the sizable deposit needed as down payment for a property. The search committee located several possible places. Some properties were located in Brixton, Tooting Commons, and Hearne Hill, which seemed ideal, as many of our members resided in Brixton. However, the doors closed in various ways on all but one, a Doctor's office at 67 Melfort Road in Thornton Heath, Surrey, near Croydon.

We had nearly overlooked this property, as it was listed 3-4 thousand pound below the market value. Our staff thought it would be probably be in disrepair.

However, we were continually drawn to the ad on this property, which lingered in the for sale ads for several weeks. On our next day off, Dorothy and I decided to drive by the Melfort Road building. From the outside, it looked well kept, so we made an appointment to view it that afternoon. Low and behold, it was in an immaculate, freshly decorated, move in, condition. The Doctor owner was retiring to the south coast, and wanted a quick sale. After meeting with us, he also made us an offer we could not refuse.

He offered to carry a private, very low interest note, if we could pay at least a one-third down payment. This meant we would not need another lender nor did we have to arrange an outside mortgage. Wow, what a God we serve! Isn't that just like our God! He really announces very clearly that this is HIS plan, with all the steps neatly worked out in advance to suit the need of the hour! Of course, the mission board agreed to a purchase under those fully agreed upon terms. We drew up the contracts and got them registered through a solicitor (lawyer).

In September 1970, the new "Christians in Action Training College" was dedicated by Lord and Lady Cyril Black, Board members of the Billy Graham Association, UK. We had met them at a Crusade at Earls Court in Wimbledon in 1966. Rev. Howard Jones, of the Billy Graham Association, (The same Howard Jones in whose home we had stayed while in Liberia), had been the guest speaker for our First Brixton graduation. He invited us to be special guests and meet the London team and Dr. Graham and his wife. This we happily did and were blessed to know and meet such an inspired team.

Lord and Lady Black expressed a desire to assist us in anyway they could, and were delighted to be invited to participate in dedicating our new outreach and discipleship training program in the Croydon, Surrey area. It was our privilege and pleasure to have fellowshipped with this gracious spirit-filled couple. Their foundation made an annual donation to the school for a many years.

Five years later, they returned to see our progress and addressed our Tenth Anniversary service at the annual European Conference of 1975. You will note that sometimes I use school and college interchangeably but in England, any classes above high school level are classified as a college whether accredited or not.

We planned the annual regional conferences with great joy and excitement. It was a time of refreshing and fellowship for the missionaries. They only had to make their way to England, and stay at the college, as we didn't charge them room and board. God supplied the needs every year, without fail!

Beginning of London Ministry

Staff 1966

36 Lancaster
Rd

Arrival in UK

Clyder Hall
Fellowship
Our first
Church
In Britain

Hospitality

Choir from RAF Base Greenham
Commons

Ladies
Fellow
Ship
Serves
the
Potluck

# Dedication of the
## Melfort Road Bible College

67 Melfort Rd, Thornton
Health, Surrey

Lord, Sir Cyril, and Lady Black dedicated
at the Bible College

# Clyde Hall Church

Taylor
family
arriving
for
service

At Clyde
Rd

Former CinA President, Rev. Lee
Shelley® at 1968 Conference in
London.

Christians in Action
European Missionary
Conference - 1970

Missionaries representing over
nine countries attended the
conference.

Our Family in London 1965-80

Taylor Family 1970

Son, Willis & friend Tom, Playing for
youth choir at Parkview Church, 1976

# Part Five
## Chapter 32

### The European Ministry Explodes and Expands

At this time, CinA had expanded throughout much of Western Europe, Africa, and into North India. Europe. There was a great movement of the spirit to target those regions in the 1970s as our missionaries fanned out across Europe, to teach evangelism classes and assist established churches in their outreach programs. The response to this recruitment brought a flood of students from across the US, daring to go out and join God's army of missionaries. This was a blessed field, as God poured out his spirit upon us with many beautiful and talented workers joining hand in hand with us as a mighty army of God.

The following chart lists the expansion of the European, Africa, and India fields from the opening of Sierra Leone in 1969 to 1979. The numbers listed are the recorded ones from the London Regional Headquarters for those dates.

| | |
|---|---|
| Macau | 4 |
| India | 2 |
| Sierra Leone | 9 |
| Spain | 5 |
| Italy | 3 |
| France | 4 |
| Germany | 6 |
| Switzerland | 2 |
| Ireland | 2 |
| England | 20 |
| Totals | 57 |

During this time, the Clyde Road Church hosted all European conferences. The missionaries were housed at the Lancaster Road property, then later at 67 Melfort Road, Thornton Heath, Surrey. God enriched our ministries as many of the grand old saints such as Anna Todd from Ireland would share about winning "Teddy Boys" for Jesus.( Teddy Boys were the gang bangers of their day. They preceded the IRA in Northern Ireland); and Martha Fritz and Grace Brackett shared on their ministry in Germany. Each team would share their most recent adventures, outreach results, and the prayer challenges of their work. Our hearts were uplifted as we saw God's hand working in each team, in many varied ways.

# The Teams under our Leadership in Europe from 1965 to 1978

## Northern Spain

Dale and Janice Simpson and four sons, along with Shirley Cash, developed a thriving church in Santander, Northern Spain. This was when Protestants were not welcomed in most of Spain, and there was lots of unrest among the Basque people.

**Tony and Carmen Aldapo,** an American Latino couple, who had formerly worked in Mexico, planted four churches in Seville, Southern Spain. They were outstanding soul winners, church planters, evangelists, and street preachers.

## The French Team

Gerald Huston, served as school dean in London for four years, but felt called to reach the people of France with the Gospel. After marrying a missionary staff member, Betty Orme, they commenced deputation for France. In 1971, they opened a base station, in Grenoble, where Roger and Dianne Smalling later joined them. They discovered that the French showed little to no interest in spiritual thing, and it was a very expensive place to live. However, through the opening of a stall for selling Christian books, they were able to maintain themselves, and reach many French people with the Gospel. This was a wonderful new ministry approach for that time, for today, this type of ministry it known as a tent making ministry.

## The Team to Italy

Tom and Irene Hodges, with their two children, sailed to Italy in the fall of 1967, where Virginia Straughn later joined them. .For over four years, this team witnessed and taught salvation through Christ and Christ alone. However, Italy was not a friendly field for Protestants and they found much hostility to their family. While visiting them in1974, Elgin discerned their discouragement, and invited them to come and join the British staff. Tom, who had been a civil engineer before becoming a missionary, was a gifted teacher, so would be an asset in the school. Thus began a close thirty-year relationship with the Hodges family, which remains via e-mail to this day.

## Ministry to Women of the UN in Geneva, Switzerland

A French Canadian, Evelyn Tedford, and a Texan, Martha Ingram, fused together into a mighty team in Geneva. Martha completed her studies in Long Beach, when Elgin served as the dean of students in 1964. Evelyn was on furlough and gearing up to return to Geneva. Martha wanted to minister in Europe with women, but hadn't decided where. Since they were single and alone, I called them together and counseled with them. Later I suggested that they unite and work together. This was to keep from sending out single women with no prayer support.

Upon arrival in Geneva, they organized weekly, lunchtime, Bible studies among the many nationalities of the UN. Classes were in English and French with hundreds of women passing through their discipleship program and completing the Navigator's courses.

Evelyn was an outstanding teacher and councilor. She had come to Christ under the ministry of Oswald J. Smith in Toronto, and in 1956 became a missionary Being very small of statue she was called "little dynamo," because of her determination and dedication to ministry goals.

Martha, a widow, had dedicated the remaining days of her life to winning women around the world to Christ. She saw many of her dreams fulfilled on the field in Geneva.

## Northern Ireland

In visiting Ireland, I usually spoke at the "Mustard Seed Mission, on Shank Hill Road. The congregation was mostly mothers, young children, and youth. Challenging them towards loving their Catholic neighbors was my focus, for the hate language and message expressed weren't the best Christian testimony. However, we found the people had grown up with this anger and hatred, similar to the problems toward Black people in the Southern US. Thus, it wasn't something that would change instantly.

My wife and I made numerous trips to visit Anna at "The Mustard Seed Mission." On one such visit, British Soldiers stopped Anna and Dorothy while they were returning from a women's meeting. The soldiers told Anna, "You must turn around and find another route." She replied, I must go this direction or it will take me hours to get home." "Well," said the soldiers, "You may not get home at all, if you proceed, for there is a

15 pound bomb in the road just a hundred yards ahead." Of course, they immediately turned around. However, because Anna had to drive to her home in Lisbon, another Town South of Belfast, she asked Dorothy if she wouldn't mind taking a bus that would drop her right in front of the home where we were staying. Dorothy, not knowing the local situation, answered in the affirmative, so Anna saw her onto the next bus.

When my wife arrived at the host home, the woman of the house inquired, "Where is Anna? " I did not hear the car." "I came by bus," Dorothy answered. "My, oh, my," said the hostess, "It isn't safe to ride a bus at night here; the IRA is hijacking and burning buses every evening."

We realized God had really had a hand and protection over Dorothy that night, first in bypassing the bomb, which blew up five minutes later, and then on the bus, for the morning news headlines read, "*Three killed as four buses hijacked and burned last night.*" We left shaken and grateful for safety.

## Underground Church in Romania

During this time, underground ministry in Eastern Europe was in its infancy. The California Board commissioned and sent to us in Europe an Eastern European couple. They were going to Romania, via London. Paul, a Russian, and his wife, a Czechoslovakian, were leading the team for this exciting new ministry; and two of our young women joined them, (Linda Vance (Ewert) and Dianne Powers (Smalling). This was a very hush, hush operation with little or no publicity announcing their ministry. We were given little information on the couple. Upon their arrival in London, we learned what gifted and exciting people they were in the ministry.

We gladly sent them to Eastern Europe with our blessings. Their ministry flourished and amalgamated with several other groups, working underground at that time for safety reasons. A year later, the two single women returned to England and Linda became my personal secretary, at the London Regional Office. Dianne met and married Roger Smalling and they helped spearhead a ministry in France.

## The British Headquarters Team

All but two of our first European conferences were hosted at the Clyde Road Church. The missionaries housed at the Lancaster Road property were later housed at the present headquarters, at 67 Melfort Road, Thornton Heath, Surrey.

It was an established policy at the time that all teams going to Europe and Africa, would go via London, their regional headquarters. It was a great arrangement, as the London staff met them and they were acquainted with our team. It also eased the missionaries into cross-cultural values. We could assist them to avoid saying they are doing it backwards or wrong. Instead, they were taught to say they are doing things differently. This was an area, which really offended the British, as they felt that they had long established customs, which they felt the Americans had changed, therefore they were justified in being outspoken regarding such issues.

So many people passed through the London Headquarters, that we are afraid to name names, for fear of leaving out a few. However, since we have already named a great number, it would be remiss of me not to at least try naming some of those who served so valiantly.

The first staff team at Lancaster road began with Caroline Rotz; Gerald Houston; Grace Brackett; Gertrude Ruiz; and Dorothy and yours truly.

At Melfort Road additional staff were added, and subtracted, as most moved on as they were called to various fields of ministry. A great problem to have!

Long serving staff members were: Bookkeeper and Assistant Pastor, Leslie Leeder, first secretary, Patricia Mills, office manager, Elaine Weston; teacher and Director for a time, Tom and Irene Hodges.

Later there were Photographer, Paul, and Susanne Powers, Personal assistants and food management, Joy and Leonard Rosenfield. Two families served as Directors during the transitional period, Ted and Caroline Martin, and Dale and Janis Simpson.

Missionaries who came to London for short periods:

From Canada: Harvey and Gloria Guenther; Vic and Mary Peters, who went to Sierra Leone; Dennis and Ruth (Barg) LeCoursier (in Peru), Marvin and Linda Ewert.

From the USA: Ginger Powers, Vanessa Lee (Daniels), Dorris Porter (Nagaujai), Daisy Russell, Donna Tolley, Bertha Green, Freddie and Wanda Roberson, Charles Hill, and Mary McKelvy.

From the UK: Anita Johnson, Joy Johnson, B.J. and Brenda Joseph, Graham and Sue Dodds, John and Sandra Levy, Susan Ng, Miriam Christie, and Vivian Johnson (Barrett). Along with many more, whose names I may not have listed here, but God remembers their labor of love to him.

A new ministry to Japan was also launched from London. The church that had sent Masaru to Long Beach years before now sent another young leader, Toshio Sato. This was an incredible person; he adjusted to the culture well, studied long hours, and could almost out hit me in baseball. I knew you needed that bit.

On holidays, the entire church went to various parks to celebrate. Baseball or soccer was always played, but before Toshio arrived, I was delegated to be empire. They said it was not fair to have only one long ball hitter and he play for one side. Sometimes I was the designated hitter for both sides, just so I could participate. After Toshio's arrival, we had highly competitive games. Recently we visited Tochio who is pastoring a large church in Kyoto, with a fantastic ministry to the Jews. They send students to the Hebrew University in Tel Aviv, where they learn the language and ministry love to the Jewish people.

While in Kyoto, I taught in their Seminary and two churches, greeting them and singing one of the many songs Dorothy and I knew in Japanese. Toshio translated as we both shared a word.

Another special family we should remember here was John and Josie Arnott and their son Fraser. Josie came to Christ during our 1972 conference. Dorothy had made a huge sign on a white sheet saying "Reach out 74" giving dates and times. She tied it to the church fence to advertise the meetings. A short windy rainstorm arose, blowing the sign down and ripping it. Josie walking by pushing two year old son, Fraser, picked it up washed and mended it and returned it to the church that evening. One of the Missionaries, Dale Simpson spoke to her and led her to Christ. Afterwards, she attended the remainder of meetings.

This was the beginning of the Arnotts relationship with God and us. Josie became an untiring worker and singer in the church. Her son, Fraser grew up in Sunday school and youth group. John, who has not publicly

119

accepted Christ into his life, at this writing, attends special meetings at the church and is not antagonistic against spiritual things. They have always invited us to stay with them whenever we are in England. We are still praying for John's conversion, very soon. God has healed him of wide spread colon cancer through long-term treatment (2 years) and much prayer, God isn't finished with him.

Lastly, at this writing, the present Director for the British Isles: Freddie and Wanda Roberson: and their ministry team members are Leslie Leeder, and Ken and Yvonne Wiebe. The Robersons are from Carson, California and are the only other Afro- American couple in our mission today. Please continue to pray for Afro-American Missionaries to serve outside the U S. Most of all, we would say pray for their acceptance by others on the field as being worthy to serve, worthy of honor and respect, and finally, worthy enough to support.

We actually observed Christians supporting Muslim workers and paying them to pass out Christian literature, in place of using Black Christians for the task. They saw the Blacks as threats to their position as leaders; hence, they would not work with them.

We also had a Jewish ministry in north London, Greta Green area, headed by Gary and Eileen young for four years.

# Chapter 33

## Purchasing the Parkview Church in Addiscombe

The training center was now settled, however, we were maintaining the lease of the church hall on Clyde Road for Sunday services. The foundation which owned the hall, were expanding their camps ministry, and began storing more and more of their tents, boats and other equipment in the hall. Our membership was growing also, and we were requiring more Sunday school and nursery space.

If you have ever rented a place for worship, you will understand what it means to have to clear away the owner's things before services each week. This arrangement was requiring more and more of our time on Saturdays to prepare for Sunday Worship. Again, the church began to quietly inquiring of buildings for sale of lease on a long-term basis in the area.

On Easter Sunday 1969, Dorothy and our three sons attended a church within walking distance of our house, when we lived on Sefton Road in Addiscombe. Elgin was on a driving tour of the European fields, and Yugoslavia, with CinA President, Rev. Lee Shelley. Our family had moved out of the Lancaster Road property to make room for the increasing student body. Dorothy was also ill with respiratory and chest difficulties. Her Asthma had grown increasingly more challenging while in the damp basement of the school. We hoped that the move to a smaller house and less stress would help her. The weather being overcast and damp in England increased her breathing difficulties, along with that of Willis.'

My family was appalled by the sparse attendance on Easter Sunday! Only twelve people attended, including themselves. After service, Dorothy approached one or two persons as to the reason there were so few. An East Indian brother, who had led much of the service, stated that it was very sad, but they were closing the church and uniting with another fellowship the following month.

Dorothy inquired concerning the future usage of the property. Well, he said, "We don't know what we will do with it, as nothing has been decided." Looking at the nicely designed and compact church, Dorothy thought, "How our congregation would love to have a place like this for worship services."

Excitedly, Dorothy shared this information with me immediately after my arrived home. The church needed to relocate so we would inquire to what arrangements could be made. As God would have it, the head elder for the denomination, which owned the church property, was a long time donor of the mission.

Bro. Roderick was the local wholesaler, where we purchased our supplies for the college. Immediately, he announced that we could lease the property for six months, while the church decided on its future plans. They even allowed us to move in two weeks before the contract was finalized, because our lease at Clyde Road had ended.

The college and church were under different financial structures, but some of the donors overlapped. Therefore, we didn't want to over burden them with overwhelming financial obligations, so leasing seemed the proper step for now. Four months into the lease, the church board decided to approach the owners once more regarding the purchase. A special church business meeting was called, and the elders and members all affirmed it was time to make an offer if the price was right, we should again, "Expand our tent."

As God would have it, when we approached their Elder Board, they gleefully agreed to sale us the building and take it off their hands, as they were still obligated for all repairs and upkeep. They put a value of L25, 000 on the building ($75,000). That seemed very low, so we verified that this was not an error and no zeros were missing. Again they repeated the same offer, and stated that they wanted us to purchase the church and use it for God's Glory, hence the low price.

Everyone joined in the fundraisers. The women's department held a large rummage sale. The men held three Saturday morning breakfasts. The youth had a sponsored walk. They chose to walk from the Brixton Market to Parkview church, a distance of approximately 12 miles. They worked hard getting family and friends as sponsors. The walk was a resounding success, the parents volunteered to set up water stations along the route; provided cars as rest stops; prepared light snacks; and even walked along side their children as encouragement. In the final stage, they also provided a big celebration meal!

This time, we were able to use the four years renting of Clyde Hall as a credit reference. We applied to Barclays Bank and secured low interest loan for 15, 000 Pounds. Needing one other reference, we approached the Doctor from whom we purchased the Melfort Road property and he verified our payment record. We had only three months left on the college payments. All sorts of scriptures came to mind on the faithfulness of our God, working through His people, for the benefit of the whole body.

In Print the glorious miracles of God sound so simple and easy, however, being there and taking those giant steps of faith weren't nearly so simple. With us, it was as stated in II Cor. 6:10, "As poor, yet making many rich; as having nothing, yet possessing all things." There were no high salaries to depend on; we had more missionaries than members attending our services. God gave us the faith to move ahead with this agreement.

As a family, we had the lowest income of all the missionaries and most of the church members. We were not paid a salary as the pastor, due to this being a mission church with very little income at that time. Our average income while in London was $600 per month. God performed as many miracles in our personal family life as he did in the ministry. Our personal life's verse is Matthew 6:33 "Seek ye first the Kingdom of God, and all these (earthly things) will be added unto you."

Daily we saw God add many things to our household. When we made sacrifices for the ministry for the church purchase, God always blessed our home as well. First, he supplied us with a very low rent house at Sefton Road in Shirley Hills, for L100 ($280) per month, the pound had dropped to $2.80. When the school building was purchased, we made large faith promises and paid them off along with the rest of the church members.

Our landlady announced during the October harvest Thanksgiving that she was putting our house up for sale. We considered buying it, but decided against that, since it needed major repairs due to bomb damage from WWII. Our family discussed the issues and prayed together over the best place to live. We decided on Thornton Heath, near the school, as we spent most of our time there.

During our family devotions, we sort God for the funds needed for the deposit. In the mean time we were told to open an account with a Building Society, so we could have a better opportunity for a loan when we found a house. So we opened an account with a about L25 pounds ($60).

Back in California, one of our donors, Captain Napoleon Weaver, had re-enlisted in the Marines and they give you a big bonus each time you re-enlist. At the end of the month, he had sent us half the tithes from that money. It arrived too late to send out in the December check.

We wrote and mailed a special fund letter, stating the need to move due to the pending sale. Two other families sent special gifts that, as God would have it, met the exact need. In April 1970, we moved unto our own house on Woodville Road in Thornton Heath, Surrey.

# Chapter 34

## The exciting arrival of Michael Edward

In the midst of fundraising for the school and then purchasing our own house, we discovered that we were expecting again. At the beginning, I felt that our timing was a bit off, since we were inundated with so much moving and lifting, which was not good for my wife. We were not unhappy; in fact, we were now more settled with a new house and plenty of space in which to welcome the new arrival. Betty Orme (Houston) volunteered to assist with the cleaning and re-decorating of the house, as Dorothy was having some difficult days.

Again, our sons had hopes for a girl, but we continued to remind them that it was always a fifty/ fifty projection for a boy or girl and in our case, with families that had mostly boys. The ratio was even less. In fact, in Dorothy's immediately family, none of her siblings had girls and mine had a majority of boys. Preparations were also moving ahead for the dedication of the school premises in September, during the annual European conference.

Michael Andrew Edward made his debut on 29 July 1970.This time, the boys didn't even think about whether it was a boy or girl. They were all pleased to see the little one and right away began bossing him around; In fact, they were so busy spoiling him that mother had to shoo them outside some days.

Older brother Elgin Jr. took great care of the child. He was elated that his little brother would follow him around the house and tried to keep him entertained. He would read stories and play peek-a-boo over and over with the young Mike.

Michael is such a blessing to us. He was an active and bright little boy, keeping his brothers on their toes. One special occasion, when he was three years of age, Dorothy and I had left him in the care of Willis and Tim, who became distracted with other things, didn't listen or answer the little Mike. Being quite fearless and resourceful, Michael pull a stool up to the front door and left the house.

About a mile down the main road, Dorothy returning home by bus spotted Michael. He was walking happily along the main boulevard, having crossed two busy intersections. Pushing the button to stop the bus, Dorothy proceeded to hop off quickly, and in her haste, injured her right leg. Immediately Mike saw his mother, and ran to her.

Dorothy anxiously inquired as to why he was this far from home on his own. Mike replied, "I am going to Daddy's office to tell him that Willis and Tim aren't watching after me, like he told them." They are making lots of noise and don't hear anything I say, nor have they given me anything to eat .Due to her injury, Dorothy rang me to pick them up. Upon arriving home, sure enough, we found the front door ajar with a tall stool still there.

The two older lads were busily and loudly doing their own things. Willis was playing and singing at the piano and Tim was listening to the stereo. Neither had noticed the child was gone. Dad spent the next half hour firmly lecturing them on caring for their younger brother.

These problem-solving traits have always lingered with Mike down through the years. So much so, that he is now busy solving problems as a computer systems analysis on his present job, in Tacoma, WA.

# Chapter 35

## Establishing a Fulltime Missionary sending Program

Many students enrolled in our London College. However, some stands out in our memory more then others, and one such person was David Hall. David had been saved in East Africa while working for the British American Tobacco Co. (BAT). When entering school, he often testified, "I must take Christ back to the people in the same aggressive way in which I sold them cigarettes." After graduation, in 1968, David stayed at the school while deputizing around England. Finally, in February 1969, we saw him off to Sierra Leone, West Africa to pioneer a CinA Ministry. He and a retired English missionary, with the unusual name, Mr. English, who was visiting on short term, flew to Sierra Leone, and thus a new arena of ministry opened for us. We were now a sending board for all CinA missionaries appointed from Europe to other fields.

The following year, Philip Cheal, joined David and six months later, Caroline Rotz (fondly called Auntie Caroline) and Donna Tolley, one of six African American missionary ladies who became workers with CinA in Sierra Leone in the 1970's.

Those courageous Afro-American missionary women, who against many obstacles labored faithfully in London and Sierra Leone, making untold sacrifices, should be named here and honored for their years of service. They are, Donna Tolley, Bertha (Williams) Green, Daisy Russell, Brenda (Brown) Joseph, Vanessa (Lee) Daniels, and Dorris (Porter) Nagaujai. They all served with low and unstable funding and under appalling living conditions, endured malaria, and other tropical diseases; nevertheless, many persons came to Christ through their ministry.

Both David and Philip return to London after serving short terms on the field, thus leaving the team without male leadership. We regret that there weren't more Afro American men or African Pastors available now. Due to the attitudes of both Western and African leaders, the women weren't well received or welcomed as leaders; causing the ministry to flounder for a short time.

In 1976, The Shelley's and Taylors hosted the arrival of Allen and Donna Goerz from Canada to the field. While awaiting their arrival, with four missionaries and twenty or more church members, two goats ran out on the airport runway. This was appalling to us, for we could see the plane coming in for its landing. Several men tried running the goats off with brooms, one left but the other didn't budge. Finally, two men picked the goat up and ran off the field just as the plane taxied up. This was Allen and Donna's introduction to the field!

The Goerzs were amazing assets to the ministry. Donna played the piano; Allen did song leading and teaching. They also weren't discouraged by the hardships of the frugal means in Sierra Leone during this time. Soon they were elected as the team leaders. The following year, they were joined by fellow Canadians, Ken, and Yvonne Wiebe. Together, they trained national pastors through the Syke Street Center and encouraged them to advance their education by enrolling at the local Jui Bible College.

A new ministry was opened up in the North in Bo, and an innovated agricultural program was established for which the Woodlake Rotary club raised a special donation for seed money. This was one of our first non-church related programs. The need was there, the people were desperate for food, so we felt we should help them meet that need.

Two other couples joined the team for short terms: Vic and Mary Peters and their three children, Nellie, Ricky, and Randy, from BC, Canada, went out in 1978 and worked with several of the churches for two years. Vic was an experienced pastor and teacher, and Mary worked with the Children's ministry.

In 1982, Chico and Vanessa Daniels and their son, Derrick, another Afro-American couple, remember them from the London report. They were commissioned in California, and sent out to work with the Kissy Church. For over three years, they did an outstanding job and helped the church move into its own property. Vanessa sang and helped with the Sunday school program. Upon their return home, they decided not to return to Africa.

By the end of 1995, there were twenty churches established around the Freetown area, with excellent pastors and teachers. Nevertheless, the following year ushered in a great civil war, which lasted for five years, bringing confusion and death. In the height of the fiercest fighting, we helped over a 200 workers and church members flee by boat to the Ivory

Coast, raising funds to help support them there for over fifteen months. After the war, some returned, but many immigrated to America, Europe, and other countries.

# Chapter 36

## Second Wave of Expansion in Europe

During the 1970's the ministry began to grow throughout Europe. It got under way; with a US Air force Tech. Sergeant, and his wife, Al and Pearl Botts. They drove from Southern Spain to attend our Summer Outreach Program. Al was a gifted preacher, and talented musician and soloist, thus making a tremendous impact on our congregation.

By word of mouth, several other US military persons began to contact us. I was invited as the guest speaker at military bases through out the British Isles, beginning at Lakenheath and Milddenhall, near Bedford. The base Commander welcomed me and took me on a tour of the facilities. While we were riding together, he inquired of my ministry in London. As explained how we had arrived from Nigeria in 1965, he stopped me and said, "I am the person who refused to allow you a visa to Nigeria! I was in national security in Washington, DC at that time. We were not permitting any visas to be issued to US Citizens due to the pending civil war. How you got the one from Liberia, we don't know. I remember it because that was my first time seeing a black missionary family on the list. That was an amazing revelation to me, for we didn't know that the authorities in Washington had a lot to say into our going into other countries, unless they were hostile to our citizens.

The Botts were transferred to England from Spain, and stationed at RAF Greenham Commons. They established a ministry on base and planted a church among service personnel. The church plant came under the supervision of CinA Missions. My family and I would drive down the last Sunday of each month as the local supervisors. We also had a quarterly joint meeting in which the chapel members would drive to the Church in Addiscrombe.

This was an exciting time for all; for Parkview Church; as they were uplifted by the Americans and their choirs; For the Americans; for they got off base and experienced what the real Britain was like.

On the American bases, it was like Little America. They only dealt with their own people; eat their own foods; and etc. Coming to Croydon, they mingled with persons of many cultures. During this time, we had over seventeen different nationalities in our congregation. This we discovered during the arrangements for the 10th Church Anniversary. The committee in charge made a flag and photo board with all the persons and their countries of birth.

A very cute incident happened during the service as we were presented the board. There were three persons from mainland Japan in our church. However, there were five Japanese flags. As we enquired, as to who were the other two Japanese Citizens, our two elder sons just sit and grinned at us! You see in Britain, you are called a citizen of where you were born. Our sons, Willis and Elgin Jr. were listed on the board as Japanese, since they both were born there.

Many new converts and contacts were disciples of this ministry, some of whom are heading up their own ministries today, to name a few, Rev. Tim Brown (San Antonio); Reverends Frank and Madeline Broadwaters (Newport Beach, VA); and Chico and Vanessa Daniels(Grand Rapids, MI) and many others.

A Major, who was the Chaplain at RAF Chicksands, invited me to become part of an outreach to US Servicemen across Germany. The Civil Rights movement was at its height and they wanted to have more Afro-American participates. I was also to be an advocate with the many ethnic groups to assist in racial harmony. This didn't pay much, but it provided free travel and all expenses paid. This was a Godsend, as my fares were covered to visit the fields I was already supervising.

On the Head Chaplain's directives, I was flown to Frankfurt Main, on the second Wednesdays to head up "Monthly Jesus Rallies" during the summers of 1972 -1974. On the weekends, Dorothy would be brought out to join me and we were flown back home on Sunday Evenings.

Many decisions were made for Christ and I made great contacts during this time. One of the most amazing and gifted preachers that I met was Pastor Gene Weathers from Suitland, Maryland. He pastored a 5,000-member church, and was an outstanding speaker, singer, and people-loving person. God greatly used him in Germany, and everywhere he was called to minister.

When the crusades closed, He approached me and requested that I become his mentor, and began sharing some vital prayer needs in his life. We prayed together, and he proceeded to make a deeper commitment toward a closer spiritual walk with Christ. Over the next five years, he sent for me at least four times to come out to Washington DC; teach his leadership classes, to a time of fellowship with him and his family.

Not knowing his many challenges, Dorothy and I fellowshipped with his family and encouraged them in their family life, prayer life, and ministry. Twice, Pastor Gene took short-term missions teams to Mexico with us. A missions and local outreach program was started from his church.

In 1998, my heart was deeply saddened, when this man of God, grew silent. Then, fifteen years, from our first meeting, Gene died an early death. I know you are thinking, "why include this in your book?" I wanted to insert this as a tribute to the memory of my son in the Gospel, Rev. Gene Weathers.

## CinA Germany Opens in Wurzburg

In the meantime, the crusades in Germany opened the door for us to plant a permanent ministry there. Two CinA missionaries had worked in Frankfurt Main before, Martha Fritz and Grace Brackett.

An Army Chaplain invited me to send a team of missionaries to do outreach on a regular basis. My personal assistant, Linda Vince, had recently married a German-Canadian, Marvin Ewert. They were commissioned to West Germany in the spring of 1975. They worked with the chapel program and started an all-German speaking service for over a year. When a new chaplain was appointed, they decided to relocate off the base.

The Ewerts were joined a few months later by two single men, Terry Moeller and Rocco Pintapinto, who planted churches in Wurzburg and Swienefurt. There are also two African churches established by Ghanaian refugees, which are part of the German ministry. Terry Moeller is now the Europe, Africa and India, Director for Christians in Action.

## Off To South China

We will never forget when John and Sandra Levy enrolled in the Melfort Road College, with their young son, Robin. They were a determined couple, who knew they were called to China; and nothing distracted them from their goal. After deputation, the Levy's flew to Macau, South China, via Hong Kong. John studied the Mandarin language and established a Bible study with university students. Sandra began attending arts and crafts classes, where she developed friendships among the Chinese women.

Later she was able to visit in homes and share her faith with the women. This was a tremendously refreshing strategy, because women are one of the larger "unreached people groups," since many never leave their homes except for shopping or visiting relatives.

From this Bible study, a Chinese student, Susanne, found Christ and came to England to take the course. She returned to Macau as a full time missionary with the Levys. Today, Suzanne and her husband, John Hyrons have a striving daycare center and church in the heart of the business district.

Later the Levy's transferred to Taiwan and pioneered a new Chinese outreach. Today, they are supervising a correspondence training ministry out of Wales.

# Chapter 37

## Farewell to Britain and Europe

In 1979, the attendance was out growing the Parkview Church building, and they sort for ways to extend the right or left walls. In the meantime, through a series of events, God began dealing in a unique way with the Dorothy and me. For the first time during our ministry in London, we decided to take the family home for Christmas. We had only gone home for short summer trips before, when the boys could be taken out of school. England doesn't have the long three months summer breaks as many schools have in the USA. It became a custom with our family, to take four months furloughs every four years, by special arrangement with the local schools.

Dorothy and I became very troubled while visiting our families and friends. Like Nehemiah, who was troubled by the broken and downtrodden walls around Jerusalem, we were troubled over the appalling conditions of the inner cities of the US. A heaviness over the atrocious lack of missions awareness and evangelism in the Afro-American churches weighed upon our hearts.

Another horrific state of affairs was the alarming rate at which Muslims and other cults were winning many converts in the inner cities of the USA. Of course, this was frightening, for many of our relatives and friends children were being caught up in these new movements, without recognizing their false teachings.

We had been overseas, helping to win others for Christ and it seemed that the walls of our Jerusalem were broken, and being penetrated very easily by the enemy of their souls. We began praying against these dreadful events back home. In Europe, we were trying to reach Non-Christians for Christ, while those same Non-Christian groups were busy in our homeland penetrating deeply into our own families and in most inner cities!

The burden didn't lift, but grew heavier throughout 1979. In August, Dorothy and I flew to Texas to be part of a family reunion; God spoke again, "You must return home!" I have repeated many times, when God speaks loud and clear, as on the Smith-Barney ads, "We *listen*." Of course there are times even now, when I second guess myself over, many; many -what ifs.

Looking back I think, maybe we could have let the family remain for awhile longer, at least until the end of the first semester. But then again, I realize, No one was there to help Dorothy and the boys neither clear out the house nor do the necessary paperwork we needed in order to turn the house over to a realtor?

As God would arrange it, I visited the US Center for World Missions in Pasadena, California, while sharing my burden and desire for opening an office in the LA area, Dr. Ralph Winters, invited me to open an office at the center, and Mrs. Tolley offered us an apartment on Fair Oaks Blvd. to rent for as long as needed.

With this in mind, I returned to London, not sure how to break the news to my wife and family. I knew they would understand, also I didn't know how they would accept the urgency of the move. Having been together with me a long time, as well and having spiritual discernment to read when God is moving, Dorothy had already begun the sorting our things and preparing to do what ever God led me to do. Our sons had questions, with this being the end of the first semester of school.

The London Church was shocked that I would even consider returning to America. They had thought I, as the founder, would always be there as pastor. However, they slowly accepted that God was leading us into a different direction.

Many of the older members and pastor friends came by the house in droves to see us and to make sure they had the news correct. Upon hearing it directly from us, they still thought it was a temporary change and that we would soon return to London.

We had much to do; sell furniture; dishes; books, and the car. There wasn't enough time to sell the house for it takes at least three moths to do the title search on most properties in Britain. We placed the house in the hands of an agent and also left a key with John and Josie so that they could tend to any leaks or other matters. The house sale was finally completed in April, five months after we left.

The church held a very emotional, heart-rending farewell for us. You would have thought it was a funeral without a coffin. All our long-term friends voiced their sadness in seeing us go, even though we announced that we would be back for the annual anniversary.

Early the next week, December 15, 1979, four members of our family, Tim, Michael, Dorothy, and I, left London. We planned to go directly to a new office at the US Center for World Missions, in Pasadena, California.

Our eldest son, Elgin II, 20, had been on his own for three years; Willis, 16, had moved over to the Melfort Road College, so he could finish Grammar School and study for "A" level exams (similar to first year Junior College). He was to join us in California upon completion of his exams.

# Chapter 38

## Founding of Global Ministries

Tim and Mike were excited about moving to California because they had visited and liked it while on furlough. Visiting a place and actually living there is very different. First the schools weren't as structured as the British had been, the children less well mannered; and drug users and pushers were everywhere on Fair Oaks in Pasadena, California, at that time. The apartment was very small and noisy, being on the second floor right over a major street.

One of the super things according to the boys was living across from a gigantic warehouse that made floats for the Rose Parade. By arriving in December, that put us there in time to see them design those beautifully decorated flowered creations and float them down Colorado Blvd. on New Years' Day.

The Rose Parade was spectacular, and we had front row viewing by observing the Police arrangements before the parade. The crowds would be all along the streets, but the side streets were kept open until just before the parade. If we arrived two streets down just ahead of the parade, we would be the first ones to fill in that street opening. It really worked well, since we lived nearby and didn't have a car to park.

At the US Center for World Missions, we were welcomed and introduced to Dr and Mrs. Ralph Winters and one hundred other ministries. I rented an office and my wife and I decorated it in lovely grays and light blues. Dorothy also designed and printed several leaflets and flyers with the name of our newly organized ministry.

We chose the name "Global Ministries" for we wanted it to be as worldwide as our present ministry. Our mission statement was -To mobilize Black churches towards mission awareness and recruit more Black individuals for world missionary service.

Our headquarters in Long Beach donated two nice desks and some older office equipment. They also agreed to pay the rent for six months, since we were representing a new branch of the same organization. We had a complete operation with our own board. We felt this was necessary for accountability as well as to give the group some autonomy in their own decisions.

Several who had shown interest came by and five members joined the board of directors, which met on a monthly basis for the first six months, but gradually, the interests begin to wane. The group realized that this required a long-term commitment and that few Black pastors were showing interest in sending people out. They seem to feel that was defeating their cause of building up their own churches.

Again, this was a new venture. The US Center had no other black organization on their campus. Daisy Russell, my secretary and I worked many long hours contacting local black pastors and inviting them to open houses at the US Center. The first time, and sometime later, several large groups attended, but few showed any major or continuing interest. We still soldiered on, believing that after repeating the cause over and over again, it would finally sink in, for we had had the same reaction in Britain. I felt that perseverance would pay off in the long haul.

We spoke and shared at Banquets, Bible studies, and Sunday services. This was wonderful for making contacts but if didn't produce more black missionaries nor did it develop the hunger in the churches that we desired to see at that time.

During this time we also be came active in several all Black organizations, such as, *The Black Evangelical Association*. We participated in their conferences and they elected us to their board of Directors in 1981-83. Then a group from Atlanta founded *Destiny*. Here was a group that we were excited for and expected great saw results. Nevertheless, it failed to move ahead and expanded too quickly for its support base.

The Mission's January conference of 1980 brought about a vast change of direction for us, again. For I had been working and living in Pasadena, CA, and traveling to Long Beach once each week to assist our Director and staff with administrative matters.

During the conference, I was approached regarding helping more at the home office. Thinking that this would just be one or two more days each week, I agreed to put my name forward. The conference voted me in as Vice President/ Assistant International Director, in charge of administration. This role was meant to be an assistant to our President, but it grew to become a major decision making appointment. Most of the ministry fell upon my shoulders, with all staff and personnel coming to my door.

Bro Lee was no longer handling major decisions at this time. We were greatly in debt and many people were being allowed free range in their departments without any oversight. As this perhaps tells you, I had my work cutout for me, when I accepted the position as Administrative Vice President/ Assistant International Director

# Elected CEO 1982

Installation Photo

CinA Conference 1982

Delegates in 1982 who elected us in as
President and CEO!

Special Presentation

To outgoing President, Lee Shelley &
Wife, Lorraine.

## The Move to Woodlake, CA

Dedication of the Ranch in 1987

Fundraising
Banquets

Dave
Konold
Becomes
Vice
President

Outreach to South India

Paul & Leila Chandran
and Family

Women &
Girls at Church

Men & Boys in the Service

# Part Six
## Chapter 39

### Elected as International Director and CEO

In September 1982, during our 25th Anniversary Conference, my name was put forward to become the new International Director and CEO of CinA. Our former director, Rev. Lee Shelly let it be known that he was retiring at age 67.

Three persons were nominated for the position, Bill Quisenberry, Phil Blankenship, and me. On the first vote, I was unanimously elected as President. At first, I stood in disbelief, but later let it be known that I wanted Bill Quisenberry to be my right hand man, as he had been my mentor for so many years. The next day, the other two candidates became first and second Vice Presidents.

Having been taught that a man's gifts makes room for him, and that if you work hard you will be respected by your peers, this then seemed more workable to me. However, real life was not that simple. It became clear over the next two years, that as an Afro person, in the USA, there were strict guidelines and barriers that you had to cross.

We chose not to make it an issue but to continue the mandate God had given us to carry on behalf of his work. We recognized that the "American Culture" would not allow for the full acceptance of "White Persons" to be publicly known as working "under an Afro-American's Leadership."

We noted with much humor, that when visitors asked to speak to the President, they would be literarily shocked to see the person behind the President's Desk was Black. In fact, I usually had to hold back a laugh since I knew what to expect. They would enter the room, look all around to see if there was someone else in the room or not.

Once a Bible distributor asked me, Are you the temporary acting President? On the other hand, is there someone else from whom I should get approval? Gleefully, I informed him that I had been elected by the missionaries as their President and I appreciated the confidence they have shown in me.

As the work grew and expanded in over twenty-three countries with church planting and relief ministry, our staff became more comfortable with us in our roles of responsibility.

This election actually became a plus for us on many fronts. In 1986, I was running meetings at an Afro-American Baptist Church in Las Vegas, and called a long time supporter of the ministry. Being an Anglo Brother, he inquired as to where I was staying, upon giving him the area, he stated, "We got to get you out of there, it's not safe over there." When he arrived, he was greatly surprised to see that I was not Anglo, and took me out for lunch.

This pastor was delighted to know that I thought highly enough of his church to call and come by, as the leader of an International Mission Organization. He stated that few mission presidents ever called or looked them up when in town, so we are able to assure him of how important his donations were to us.

## The Installation Service

We had a great installation and Silver Anniversary celebration at a local auditorium, with several celebrity guests, including the Famous Dodger's player, "Dusty "Baker, ( now Manger of the Chicago Cubs), who was the brother of our missionary in Colombia at that time, Tanya Baker Orosco.

There were presentations to the fields for outstanding work in special categories. We honored the former Director, Lee Shelley and wife Lorraine, their twenty-five years of dedicated and faithful service. They were presented with many "Silver Awards" from individual missionaries, along with a full service, silver tea set from the organization.

My being elected to the head office, was not without opposition, firstly there were those who opposed having an Afro-American leader, and some who had someone else in mind. Strongly worded messages, even a few harsh and lightly threatening, were sent directly to me. Others sent messages via friends or family, stating they would leave rather than work under my leadership. In fact, two missionary families totally discontinued any personal communication or attending conferences during the entire twenty years that I remained the Director, but the board tolerated and appeased them, rather than releasing them.

I recognized racism as being their main reason, however if you approach them, they would give very differing excuses for their actions. It also become even more suspect when the very year in which I retired, the same two families were the most visible and most vocal participants in the 2002 Conference.

Some of you will not understand why Christians, especially missionaries, who are saying they are called to win people around the world for Christ still carry such prejudices. We must all remember, we are, all, a product our past environment. If you were raised to believe that certain people are not to be respected, honored, and recognized under any circumstances, you will accept that and grow up with such a belief in your heart. This is a factor I have had to face in all societies, but much more so in the American culture, than in all others. In Britain, Japan, and Canada, people are welcomed and judged more on their contribution to society than on the color of their skin.

However, we as Americans have transported our ideals and values to other countries. Today we see other nations not willing to accept Afro-Americans as missionaries or short-term workers. So much so that we have had to prove that, they have the credentials, the experience, and tolerance for others, before they arrive in the country, a requirement that is not demanded of other races. Yet, there are many intolerant people in all cultures, and we are all required to have a "Christ centered and Christ honoring life" no matter who we are in order to give our Glory and Praise to HIM.

These circumstances faced us head on, on a daily basis, even while serving as the Director and CEO of a multi-national, intercultural, interdenominational, international, ministry. Many decisions whether personally or board driven, were always viewed as suspect until proved to work. Some persons even put up barriers in order to hinder the success of certain projects initiated by me.

In the meanwhile, I had already proven myself in Europe (one of the most difficult regions for a non-Caucasian person to work); Africa; and Asia, therefore I had confidence in approaches to ministry that I already knew would work successfully.

# Chapter 40

## Organizing our priorities

It became quite clear in the first few weeks, that there were no clear ministry priorities; therefore, we had to work through and set the following goals:

### 1. Finances

The Priority: My first action after being elected was to arrange a full audit and assessment of our financial viability. It was a great shock, as I learned we were over one hundred thousand dollars in debt, and that debt was growing rapidly on a monthly basis.

The solution: Immediately, I cut all unnecessary spending; arranged for bi-monthly accounting reports from each department and organized local fundraisers. We discovered that each department had acted independently up to this time, with separate budgets and petty cash accounts. However, this encouraged the left hand not to know what the right hand was spending and vise versa. Each department was given a monthly amount and any funds carried over, were left in that department, and became discretionary funds for that department to use as they saw fit.

The formal action: It seemed good to have the department use its allotted funds monthly, but it meant that when another area needed extra, there were no organizational records to indicate any funds being available, even through some departments did have monthly surpluses. Therefore, we chose to pool all resources and pay all expenses from one common source, the accounts department. This also allowed us more flexibility and accountability for things purchased.

The other issue of accountability, was not knowing what was the organizations property and what was individual's. Some things were listed as on load from certain persons and we needed more set boundaries. People began to come and request the return of many items, stating that such things as chainsaws, tools, kitchen equipment, and desks were their personal property. In the end, we allowed many things to move on as we had no proof one way or another to whom they belong.

From this experience, we took inventory and made lists of all Mission property, thereby eliminating such uncertainty in the future. A practice that I believe is being continued today.

## 2. New Staff

New staff was required to fill some of the necessary offices. One such person needed was a full-time bookkeeper. Doug and Becky Sutherland were home on furlough from Macau, South China, and because they were expecting another child, were not returning immediately to the field. I approached Doug on checking the accounts and helping me in the reorganizing of that department.

Doug agreed, provided he could take a short course in bookkeeping, as he felt he lacked the skills required for such a ministry. I might add here, Doug became a great bookkeeper and did an excellent and outstanding job for ten years, before transferring to the Philippines Ministry, which he has been forced to discontinue due to illness. Our prayers are with him through his long and extensive battle with cancer at the time of this writing. *(Doug went to be with the Lord a few months after I began writing this book)*. Elaine Brightbach, a former bookeeper at the Broadway stores, also joined Doug in the in the accounting department.

Many other new staff members joined us later, such as Tom and Irene Hodges, computer department; Leonard and Joy Rosenfield, office and accounts; both families had been with us in London  And later, Dave and Beth Konold, former missionaries to Korea; Phil and Marlene Blankenship, Norma Hunt; Olivia of  Guatemala; Jim and Mariah Marquart, Colombia; and many, many more.

## 3. Operating Expenses

Our Radio and Newspaper ministries were not cost effective, but we kept both of them for two years, mostly as advertisement than for income. Gradually, we discontinued the Radio broadcast on KGER, as it was the greatest drain of our limited resources, with very little financial results. Sometimes, I would look back and wish we could have kept the broadcast going, as getting a space on such a well-known Christian station became more difficult. However, that was the best thing to do at that time.

Sure, we wanted to keep our name before the people, and getting another prime time radio spot was almost impossible. But when you are spending over 40% of ministry funds on radio ministry, while the staff and the ministry itself was strapped for operating expenses, then the radio becomes a much lower priority.

Living in staff members were given a room plus board and $50 TO $150 PER MONTH, along with any personal support they could raise. However, they weren't given time off except Christmas and Easter to rise support

## 4. Fund Raisers

We set several financial goals for the ministry and then began holding fundraising banquets and breakfast mornings at a local Denny's with several supporting churches. I also began to travel and speak at churches, Rotary Clubs, and other Christian groups on the behalf of the organization. This effort brought several businessmen and pastors on board as friends and prayer partners.

**Later, we elected a board of Directors from this group of executives and Pastors.**

This was especially important, for I personally felt that there was the need for advisors and persons to hold the leaders accountable for their actions. The missionaries couldn't be there to know first hand what changes were being made, nor could they supervise spending practices. New rules had been made in the past without any of the missionaries being aware of those "new rules."

Boundaries and hindrances had become "law" which was "personal" ideas of a staff member rather than a Biblical mandate. Having an outside board as mandated by the State of California when we registered as a charity, really helped to steer the leadership on a straight course and bring new ideas and approaches to the ministry.

Sometimes we who are already in the ministry lose sight of the changes and new methods that are evolving in missions. Having others with a different viewpoint really helps us see new directions and methods.

A Board of Directors also gave us people of influence to speak on our behalf. We didn't always have to fly blindly or alone. The first eight persons worked so diligently along side us for over seventeen years, and showed concerned for the welfare of this ministry. They gave of their personal resources repeatedly.

*I give my personal thanks and appreciation to the long-serving board of Directors, who stood beside this organization and me.*

Thanks to the following Pastors:

- Bishop George Thornton, United Holy Church, (my old Marine buddy)
- Bishop Foday Farrar, Pastor, Solid Rock Ministries, Raleigh, North Carolina
- Rev. Vern Heidebrecht, (formerly of Neighborhood Church, Visalia, CA. Presently, he is at Northview Community Church, Abbotsford, BC, Canada, and my pastor.
- Rev. Thomas Sims, First Baptist Church of Glenarden, MD
- Pastor Marcus Roberts, Calvary Pentecostal Church, Brooklyn, NY
- Rev. Allen Rueter, Woodlake Presbyterian Church, Woodlake, CA

*Thanks and appreciation to the following Business Executives:*

- Eric Helgesen, Judge, Woodlake, Courthouse, Woodlake CA
- Mr. Robert Stiles, Builder, and mission leader with Far East Broadcasting Company
- Mr. and Mrs. Dick Carlton, Carlton Insurance of Torrance, CA
- Don Yeider, Construction Business, Torrance, CA
- Sylvester Harris, Educator, Carson, CA
- Art Penner, Postmaster, President, CinA Missions Canada.

Others joined us later but these made up the first and longest serving board members.

## 5. Pastoring the Long Beach Church

Being the CEO of an international mission is a full-time job, but trying to pastor a multi-cultural church at the same time was counter productive to the mission. There are so many requirements and demands on the Director in overseeing the fields, that pastoring hindered or prevented him from being free to travel and perform many duties that a CEO should be doing.

In the past, as European field Director, I had always tried to be there for the missionaries to advise and encourage them in their ministry. However, being a local pastor prevented me from during many of those things; therefore, I endeavored to train someone else to pastor the Long Beach church.

My mentor, and Vice President, Bill Quesinberry, was appointed as the pastor of the church. He pastored on Okinawa and in Brazil, so we felt this was a great opportunity for our local church to have an elder statesman in the pulpit. Bill and wife, Adeline pastored the church for two years, before returning to Brazil to assist their two daughters and their families there.

Here again, the "North Long Beach Community Church" was back in my hands to pastor. This time, I decided to really work with the church and see what we could develop. It became highly successful, so much so that we out grew the Market St. facility and rented the local Methodist Church for our morning services. Fortunately, for us they met at 10 am and were out by 11am. We opened at 12noon and were out by 1:30pm.

God blessed the services, with nationalities attending. There were the usual baby dedications, baptisms, visitations and sad to say one funeral. An elderly couple joined the fellowship for a few months and the wife passed away. Mostly we had young families in the church.

Believing that I really needed to be free from pastoring to visit the many missionaries on the fields, we appointed another pastor. Over the next six months, the services began to dwindle and dry up. Whereas they requested our return, we knew that we could not. The carrying of a church and full-time mission was more than I felt able to carry indefinitely.

# Chapter 41

## Women's Ministry Organized

After being at the headquarters for eight months, Dorothy became concerned that the women had no special ministry. She inquired of the women, would they attend a monthly meeting especially with their interests at heart? The response was over whelming, yes. Consequently, she rapidly set a date for the first meeting. She had organized the same type of meetings in the London ministry many years prior.

The opening meeting was called the President's Wife's Tea, with little tables set by missionaries from various countries. It sounded so interesting, that the church members who were not originally invited begged to be included.

Within two months, the women had large gatherings filling the cafeteria each month. This became a great outreach ministry also, as it opened to all comers and friends. Visiting missionaries spoke on their ministries, and new converts gave short testimonies of their conversion experiences. The name was change to the monthly women's meeting, with the "President's Wife's Tea" being held at the annual missionary conferences.

Of course, we men were a bit envious, as we had no such meeting. In addition, the women had food and special treats each month. Dorothy suggested we have a men's breakfast some Saturday mornings, such as those held in London. Thinking, I could start that, since I had hosted many in London, I invited everyone to come on the third Saturday for a men's' breakfast.

The response was awesome; Dorothy had to come to my rescue in making pancake dough. I could make small amounts, but when forty men showed up, I just could not stretch my mix. Later, we men organized and had a breakfast every two months.

Various forms of fellowship helped the ministry grow and helped the people become better acquainted. This is absolutely necessary when working cross-culturally. It helped us learn more about one another's culture and customs. We found that in England, the work grew, when we took the women's meeting to various homes. The women began to understand each other's strong points. As well as their limitations,

We also found several women who were great decorators and called on them to utilize their skills for the church. You do not know these things if you have no close connection with the people.

# Chapter 42

## The Property Search

The training programs, outreach, and follow up were at the Market St. facility. Then in 1984, the conference decided that we needed to relocate to a larger facility. A search committee was formed and they spent several months viewing and visiting locations for the right property.

In the fall of 1985, we learned of a camp property for sale in Woodlake, CA, by Hume lake Christian Camps. During the Thanksgiving Holidays, a large group of us caravanned up to the camp to view it. The property was beautifully situated in the foothills, just below the Sequoia National Forest home of the Giant California Red Wood Trees. There were three house and three mobile homes on the property; a large dinning room with a commercial kitchen; four large canvas Teepees that slept up to eight persons; Four bathhouses, two for men and two for women.

The campgrounds covered over 63 acres of land, with a two-story dormitory with eight rooms, and five bunk beds in each room; a waterslide down to a lake with canoes; baseball diamond; horseshoe pits and more. We visualized the possibilities of using the down stairs for offices and the upstairs for visiting missionaries. The Tepees would be utilized for the camps, along with the large dinning room and kitchen.

The staff was excited with the property and various ideas and usages were envisioned. With those thoughts in mind, we approached the Board of Directors, some of whom had gone with us to view the camp, regarding the sale of our Long Beach property and the purchase of the ranch. The Board agreed, but cautioned us that it might take a bit longer to sale our property since it was in two plots on opposite sides of the street and more of a specialized property.

Again, I have to say, Dorothy had a way of keeping abreast with local events. She noticed that a local ministry, which assisted unwed mothers, had been in the news a lot due to their lack of housing. The Pastor, Rev. Ron Howard, had taken a number of mothers to be into his church and housed them in their Sunday school rooms. This was against local health regulations.

They had been searching for a larger facility in which to house mothers and newborn babies. They mentioned receiving several donations for purchasing property, which they could use as a down payment, after selling their present property. There was a buyer and things were moving along well, however, they had not located a property suitable for their type of ministry, which would also meet the health regulations.

Knowing that our property met the health regulations and had washrooms and bathrooms available, we contacted Rev. Ron Howard of "His Nesting Place Ministries" and offered his the Market Street property at a fair market value. At first, he felt he would only needed the main building at 350 E. Market St, since it held the main offices and housing for our students. We began negotiating with Hume Lake for the purchase of their property, stipulating that our agreements would have a continuant upon the sale of the Long Beach facility. Within five weeks, we all came to full agreement and processed the documents together. By June 1986, the sell and new purchase was completed. Hume Lake was very congenial to us, when they learned that we would have to move thirteen families over two hundred miles, they arranged the moving for us. Three moving vans were sent to move all of us from Long Beach, CA to Woodlake, CA. Everyone was elated and looking forward to our new Ranch home in central California.

# Chapter 43

## A Great Tragedy

At this junction, I must pause and regress, for that is what God allowed at this point. Have you ever been in the midst of a wonderful outpouring of God's Spirit and all is moving smoothly, then Satan goes on the offensive and attacks with all his forces.

Here we were in the midst of three big miracles all the way! God has put his hand of blessings upon everything to do with the sale, the finances, and the move. We had only one more document to sign before completing everything and moving to Woodlake!

On June 14th, Dorothy and I, along with two other missionaries, Louis Soto and Bruce Rohr, drove up to complete the last formal document and even took some office furniture and a few personal items to the new property. It was an all day trip, first, to the Hume Lakes' offices, in Fresno, then meeting up in Woodlake. We decided to return home that same evening given that the property was not ready for occupancy and there being so much more to move.

Upon our arrival home, the phone rang. An excited and frighten staff member was requesting Elgin to hurry immediately to the local hospital, and asking for Louis Soto, as this emergency was concerning his wife. We knew he had left Woodlake, so thought he would be arriving soon.

Lorraine Soto, Louis' Wife, had been suffering from manic depression, along with severe emotional problems for several months. The family was in special counseling sessions, due to the wife's delicate health. Little did we know how serious it really was!

When I arrived at the Long Beach hospital, Loraine was in ICU after having ingested a large quantity of toxins while her mind was confused. I sat beside her while she whispered a prayer of forgiveness from God, her family and the Missionaries. She also expressed that her mind was in such a confused state that she could not remember taking it, or even remembered why.

In the meantime, Dorothy was calling all the contacts we knew in Bakersfield, in order to locate Louis. We were told that he had stopped to visit with a former missionaries in that area. Upon contact, He left immediately, but arrived too late to see his wife alive, she died minutes before his arrival. Their twelve-year-old daughter and nine-year-old son, along with all the other families on the compound were in deep shock. It was a sad and traumatic time.

Nevertheless, God...moved us on. The new location did wonders for the staff, as they threw themselves into the decorating and cleaning up of the "Woodlake Ranch."

Where in Long Beach, many families had lived in two rooms, now the married ones had homes of their own, and only four single women had to share two to a house.

All though the new office was small and a bit crowded, everyone knew the plan was to build another office and headquarters as soon as possible, there fore it was more bearable knowing it was only temporary.

# Chapter 44

## Developing and Expanding the Church Planting Program

For the next seventeen years, we held children's camps, retreats, and fundraisers on the ranch. God enabled us to hold banquets in Los Angeles; San Francisco; Oakland; Visalia; Fresno; San Diego; Long Beach, and Pasadena, California. We held some private banquets for ten to fifteen persons with special interest in the Ranch.

Many local churches welcomed us such as Woodlake Presbyterian; Woodlake Baptist Church; Woodlake Church of the Nazarene; and Woodlake Christian Center.

From Visalia: Grace Community Church, First Assembly, Visalia Church of the Nazarene, and Neighborhood Church. From Tulare: Mt Zion Baptist Church and from Fresno: Fellowship Baptist Church. The churches and their pastors encouraged and supported our ministry. We would show our thanks and appreciation to each one for what they did on our behalf. We had never before felt so loved and so welcome!

They also gave many of their members the freedom to help our ranch auxiliary function on the ranch. Without this army of volunteers, we would never have accomplished the task of training and sending missionaries to many fields around the world.

In three years, we were able to complete the present 7400sq ft office facility and fully furnish it. It was named "Van Dellan House" after the founder of the Ranch, Mr., and Mrs. Edward Van Dellan, who opened the ranch as an outreach to local children in the 1950's. Mrs. Alberta Van Dellan was healed of TB and promised God to give a special Thanksgiving offering to him. The offering they choose to give was the Woodlake Ranch. They originally presented the property to the *Navigators* Ministry, who in turn sold it to Hume Lake Christians Camps. We know this was quite a sacrifice but when they made a pledge to God, they followed through and kept it. We wanted to honor their vision and dedication by keeping that Christian Heritage alive.

Today this ministry, *Christians in Action Missions International*, continues to grow and expand from Woodlake and we are proud of what God continues to do through it.

As a faith ministry, they are dependant upon donations from individuals and churches to maintain the many areas of ministry, therefore we encourage those who can, to continue to support this worthy ministry.

Dave and Beth Konald served in Korea and Okinawa, for several years. In 1988, they joined our staff and Dave was elected Vice President.

Upon my retirement, Bob and Lottie Spencer, Director of Brazil ministry, joined the administrative staff at Woodlake. Today, Dave Konold head sthe ministry as President, and Bob is the Vice president.

This ministry serves in over 23 countries around the World, with various forms of outreach such as church planting, education, relief and medical teams.

# Chapter 45

## Expansion continues, Worldwide

During the twenty years that I served as CEO, I wore many hats and carried many responsibilities. Some of which included being: Teacher of Missionary Leadership Courses, Fundraiser; Conference speaker, Worldwide Church Planter; and The Developer of Humanitarian Programs in the USA, India; Canada, The Philippines; Colombia; Sierra Leone and Ghana West Africa.

Before, we had assisted other church planting ministries, but in the late 1980's it became clear that we needed to help our own converts in training; establishing; and building their own churches. So kicking off in Novaleches in the Philippines, we helped to plant four churches, assisted by Pastors Marcus Roberts, of Brooklyn, New York; and Pastor Foday Farrar, of Raleigh, North Carolina

We developed the pattern of taking teams out to run crusades in four or five villages and set up Bible studies for the converts. When the converts grew to 25 0r 30, we would assist them in building a church. Afterwards we would support the ministry for five to 10 years. As the churches grew and could support their own pastors, we would move on to another field and assist them to plant churches using the same method as model.

This method of church planting became our basic model for future expansion. Today, we continue to use it in our ministries around the world. In some regions, five years is not sufficient time for the churches to develop a support base, however, it will get them well on the way to self-reliance.

It was also in the Philippines that we expanded into ministries other than church planting. Several of the churches wanted to help the working mothers by opening *Kiddie School*. Two of the Pastors wives had credentials for childcare and they felt if would give the churches more income. Praying with the pastors, I gave my approval of the idea and gave a donation as seed money for the two projects. A year later, those projects were such a success, that they had to enlarge the churches, to accommodate the parents who had found Christ.

Later in this field, we broke with traditions and sent medical teams for the first time. Doug Sutherland faithfully led that program for many years. Teams were organized and sent annually. If I had the funds, I would set up a Doug Sutherland Medical Outreach Foundation in his memory. His loss in 2001 was a great blow to the organization and me. He had been my right hand man in accounting for so many years.

In South America, we began in Colombia, in an African village, Palenque. People who escaped from slave ships or those who fled from slave masters settled this village. The word in the Spanish language means, "Those who resisted."

We had been aware of this village for several years, as two of our former missionaries had gone there for a weekly ministry. During a Latin America Conference in 1991, Pastor Marcus Roberts and I hired a car to take us to the village.

It was amazing to me, to see "an African Village in Colombia." Walking in the town plaza, a woman approached us inquiring why we were there. We shared that Tonya Baker, one of our missionaries, had told us of this village.

The woman's eyes widen, and she asked, "You know Miss Tonya?" She led me to the Lord, many years ago. Please come and meet our chief. The chief and his council welcomed us and told us all bout their community.

Over the next two years, our Colombian team setup weekly outreaches using the village hall. There was great interest shown in the new ministry. Pastors of the other churches in Colombia helped to send out students to evangelize the area.

Pastor Roberts become motivated to train and send a full-time worker to the village. He sent a young woman to the California center, to take the training course and go out full-time.

The Colombian headquarters sent a full-time pastor from Cartagena. The work grew and a regular group of 200 people was meeting in the village hall. We returned with a team in 1993 to build a church, with funds from two fundraising efforts. Pastor Roberts purchased plans for a 350 seat-round church. The idea was exciting, for it matched the round huts of the village.

The dedication service was special to us. Dorothy and I were ecstatic to see the people rejoicing over having the only evangelical church in the area. Over five hundred people attended with many standing outside. The team shared in the service via testimonies and songs.

Today, this church is moving ahead with outreach and the woman sent from New York, is still faithfully carrying on in the ministry.

# Chapter 46

## Second Expansion in India, Kerala State

In 1978, I visited India for the first time to encourage Danny and Barbs Cherian in the Rajasthan area. We had sent them as, "tent makers" missionaries. They were to work on regular jobs and win the people through personal witness.

Being schoolteachers by profession, they opened a school near a cement plant. This work grew and was the best-rated school in the region. When other missionaries were forced to flee for their lives, the Cherians were allowed to remain.

While visiting, a Youngman named Paul was assigned as my translator. Paul Chandran was keen on things of the Lord. He had the drive and fortitude to make a great leader. As we prepared to fly back to England, he approached me about our college in Thornton Heath. I gave him two brochures and asked him to send in an application.

In 1980, Paul arrived in London after we had transferred back to the US. He completed the training was commissioned in 1981 to Kerala, State, South India.

When the work expanded and we were taking teams, Kerala was one region selected. Pastor Farrar and a large team from his ministry, and my wife and I traveled out to help Paul.

They had set up the crusade on a large banana plantation. The first night, over a thousand people gathered, with only women and children sitting down. The men were in a circle around the outside. In asking Paul why the men were not inside the center section, he looked at the seating and said, "There are no clear barriers between the men and women." We will put a rope down the center and then, the men will come. It was amazing to see that none of the men would sit anywhere near the women.

The next evening the numbers increased to over sixteen hundred, and as I stood up to speak, a Hindu Priest with a drummer and bell ringers came right in front of meeting place, to ward off the "evil" spirit. Standing quietly and praying until they passed, I told the group that the adversary was busy and we had to pray for them. They moved on and we had a marvelous service.

164

When the invitation was presented, over 400 people came forward. I called for the pastors and workers to gather around and pray for them. We noticed that no one moved from in front of me. Speaking to the translator, I asked why the other pastors were not coming and praying with the people. He informed me that in India, the people believed that the "Holy man" as they called their teachers, was anointed to give the message therefore, he was anointed to lay hands on them. My back was giving me problems during this trip, and I really dreaded having to pray over everyone, somehow, we made it!

On the last night of the crusades, an extremely handsome man approached me as I was leaving the grounds. "Hey, teacher," he said in English, "I want to take your God! The Americans' Gods are good they help make them rich."

Turning around, I begin asking him if he really knew who Jesus was. No, he replied, I just heard the talk (message). I quietly took him aside and began to show him the different between the dead gods of the Hindu; Buddha; and Mohammad, in comparison to the risen redeemer, Jesus. With tears, that young man accepted Christ as his savior and Lord.

The next day we discovered that he was a famous movie actor in India, named Ballaruma Babu. He had told me to call him Babu. He attended one other meeting. Paul told us that he and several members of his family joined his local church for over a year, before moving to Bombay. We have not been back to India for many years now, but thank God for the ministry there. Paul has built two Orphanages, a seniors home, and twenty churches.

## North India

As mentioned before, Danny and Barbs Cherian opened a school in the north in 1974. Danny, who was born in the region, died on the operating table during gall bladder surgery. Pray for wisdom for his widow, who is continuing the ministry. We are praying for people who will go and help minister the Word in India. Many persons from the Western world travel to India to learn Yoga and other eastern customs, why not have Christians, going out to carry the Truth and the Way! India is a country so steeped in religion that everything is becomes a "god."

We had an experience in Mumbai (Bombay) which we shall never forget. There was a religious festival on when we arrived. Each evening, all through the night, we heard loud noises like someone breaking things. Later in the week, we asked Paul what that banging was that kept on all night long.

Paul gave us the widest smile we had ever seem, and said, "They are trying to wake up their Gods so he can hear their prayers. That was when we understood why Paul had such a wide grin. He said, "Can you imagine hitting the Idol with a coconut shell to wake him up?" Those are coconut shells thrown at the idol's feet all night, this week. Next week it will be something else for the God.

We were certainly thrilled to bits that we had a God who heard us at all times and never slumbers or sleeps. We have not been back to India for many years now, but thank God for the ministry there. Paul has built two Orphanages, a seniors home, and twenty churches.

# Chapter 47

## The Move to Canada

We approached the board regarding opening a new office in Canada. We had many contacts but needed someone to develop this region. Our son, Willis, wife Nellie, and two granddaughters lived in Abbotsford, BC. We desired to be closer to them. Now that we did most correspondence with computers, we felt our work could be done from any office.

The accounting and publishing could continue unhindered in Woodlake.

The board granted us the authority to investigate the possibilities of an office in Canada, beginning in June 1995. We drove to Canada and stayed with Willis and Nellie for a month. They enquired as to where we desired to live. Nellie then suggested that we pool our resources and share a house together.

Dorothy and I were delighted that our children would be excited to have us with them. We made arrangements with them to start the proceedings towards the purchase of a large two-story house in Abbotsford on Sumas Mountain.

Returning to California, we revealed the new plans around the office. As with any move, there were the pros and the cons. Three years prior, I had given the board notice that I planned to retire at age 65. Now, three years later, no one was stepping forward to train for the position. We felt that if we moved, others would began to step up and take the reigns and fill the slots.

# Chapter 48

## The Death of Elgin Jr

In the midst of planning and expanding to Canada, we had our most devastating attack by the enemy. On Saturday, September 9, 1995, two police officers came to our home in Woodlake. Answering the door, I will never forget their message. "Rev. Taylor, you have a family emergency in Santa Ana, California, please call this number." Dorothy was out in the rear of the house, working in the flowerbeds. I called her and in and told her the Police had been there. In addition, they gave me a special number to call. She stood very still, and then asked me, "What is it?" We do not know anyone in Santa Ana. We talked to Elgin twice last night. Honey, she asked, what do you think it is?

First, we sat down near the telephone, prayed for God's guidance and peace as we made the call. I did not tell Dorothy, but the answering voice said, "Coroner's Office." I felt a pain in my chest as I enquired about the message sent by the Police.

They informed us that our eldest son, Elgin Jr, age 35, was dead! Just after he alighted from a bus in Santa Ana, California, he was shot in the crossfire of a drive by shooting. The coroner did not believe they were aiming at him, and listed the death as by misadventure. He was carrying a small sports bag with a change of clothes, and had a wallet, with his ID and Driving License, along with two tokens for the L-Train in his pockets .The L-Train station was two blocks from where he died.

We were stunned, and shocked beyond words. Surely they were wrong, perhaps someone had stolen Elgin's wallet. We had just spoken to him three times the evening before. He called home often just to chat and keep abreast of the latest family news. The coroner apologized, but said they were definitely sure of the identification of the victim. We asked about the long scar on his right elbow from an accident at age 8. "Yes, it is there" he said, and then they instructed us on the arrangements we must make.

Hanging up, Dorothy and I grabbed one another and wept over the death of our son. There is no way we can express our feelings over this lost. If you are a parent, your children are precious to you and you pour out much of your hopes and dreams into them and the future. Just as

I had few words when he was born, I again had to just sit there quietly, and reflex on his life. Consequently, we sat together, and reflected on the night before, when he had called twice speaking only to his father, then called back requesting to talk to Mom, as he had not greeted her on previous calls.

Our next actions were to break the news to our family. We called each of our three sons, Willis and Nellie, in Canada, Michael, a student in Fresno State, and Timothy in Las Vegas, NV. They were staggered by such shocking news. All three wanted to assure us that they were there for us and would be home immediately. Michael being the nearest arrived within the hour and Willis and Nellie drove through the night to be with us from Canada. Tim was working on arrangements to come.

Given that it was a weekend, we had to call our Vice President, Dave Konold at his home in Visalia, who assured us that he would notify the rest of the staff. I shall never forget our long time friend and auxiliary leader, Al Hogue, was the first to come to the house. He came with tears expressing his profound feeling of our lost.

Al had worked with our son in the maintenance on the ranch for several months when we first came to Woodlake. He gave each of us a big hug and said I really loved Elgin Jr. He was such a great worker. We shall really miss him! "We worked together on the grounds and pumps at the lake for a long time. I am so sorry!"

Later, Dave, Beth, and several staff came and sat with us and prayed for us. They all offered comfort and expressed their sincere regret of our loss. God has those special people who are just there for you, no matter what you are going through. We love and appreciate each of them.

Again, Bishop George Thornton was there. He lives in Santa Ana, so we rang him regarding funeral homes and services. He recommended one that he had used when his beloved wife, Pauline died the year before.

He also said he would meet us there the next morning. We were to arrange things with a funeral director, before the coroner would release the body.

Early Sunday morning, we drove to Santa Ana to arrange for our son's memorial service. It seemed as though it was something happening in a dream or on TV, not real, and perhaps we could awake and it not really be true. Nevertheless, the reality hits when you walk through the funeral home and have to choose a casket and flowers, etc.

Today we can speak calmly of all this. However, at the time, we were like walking zombies for several days. Just the thought of how he died would send goose pimples up our arms. We could not deal with the violence of his death.

Again, we thank God for leading Elgin all of his life. He had accepted Christ at age of nine, and showed a kin interest in spiritual things. However, having been born with a brain injury that affected his behavioral patterns, he could be erratic and uncontrollable often. Doctors told us he would not live past age 18, and all of his classmates died early, but God allowed him to live to age 35.

Elgin Jr. had an amazing life in spite of all his handicaps. He was married for eight years, no children, worked on various jobs, completed a one-year college course in *Hotel and Restaurant Management*, and worked at hotels and restaurants in both the UK and California. He worked for five years at Bank of America as a customer credit rating verifier, and was an avid reader with an extensive vocabulary.

The most wonderful thing of all, our son loved Jesus. In 1987, Elgin came to Visalia, CA after his divorce. He was lonely and disillusioned. We prayed with him and reminded him of his receiving Christ at age nine. He recalled the day and said I want to be right with God again. He entered the Victory Outreach rehab center and for the next year, we saw an amazing transformation. Elgin talked about Jesus and drove his mother to local revival meeting when I was away. This was when we really knew without a doubt, that Elgin loved the Lord. Later, he joined a ministry in Compton where he located jobs for convicts and drove a bus to take them to services at Rev. Fred Price's Church on Sundays.

On September 16, 1995, we held the most remarkable memorial service for our son. People came whom he had helped off the streets, along with many friends and family members, who knew the fun boy he had always been. We say here again, Thank you for being there to hold our hands when we needed that extra boost to carry on. Dave and Beth, Frank and Norma, Bishop Thornton, Willis & Nellie, Michael, my brother, James and Odessa Taylor, Dorothy's sisters, Louise and Alfreda, Cousins, Martha and John Alley, and lifelong - friend, Sister Anita Johnson of the UK, now living in Florida. To you, along with all the missionaries, staff, our many friends, again we say ,thank you .

After Elgin's death, we were more determined than ever to move to Canada near Willis. He was having a series of asthma attacks and we feared losing him, too. Most of all, we knew God wanted us to go to Canada. At the years' end, we moved to Abbotsford, BC. Two months later, we joined Northview Community Church, where our dear friend, Vern Heidebrecht, pastored. Our plans were to continue the Africa outreach from Canada.

In Sierra Leone, a great civil war hindered any outside outreach for four years. Nevertheless, the National Church members continued their witness and prayers. When we heard of the appalling conditions of our church people and the country, we started a 5-gallon bucket food drive. Making a list of the things to be included, we sent out the list to several churches, along with a deadline for receiving them at Northview Church. This was the most successful food campaign we have ever had. The response was so warm and rewarding, that many have asked us to have another one.

The church had every hallway filled with buckets stacked six high and still buckets were coming. One church from Seattle, drove the 200 miles to bring a truck loaded with food buckets. The idea of the buckets, was to have a ready to distribute form of distribution.

We had passed out various foodstuffs before, and found we needed a ready packaged product to avoid the mob of hungry crowd. .Before, people had punched bags, broke the plastic lids, to take a little for themselves. Now we could take each family a bucket or divide buckets for single people.

We shipped two containers of food, one from Canada, and one from America. A team went with us to meet the containers at the docks. The dock supervisors, gave us a horrible time, so much, so that I had to actual threaten to report this on CNN and say how they were keeping the people from getting food.

It was also amazing to see how the churches had flourished. Even three men who weren't Christians had assisted Christians escaping a warlord, and in the process became Christians themselves. We were so blessed to see how the people chose to feed the disabled and small children before anyone else. There was no rioting as we distributed the five-gallon food buckets sent from Canada and the USA.

The Sierra Leonean had always been a non-aggressive quiet people, but seeing small babies with their arms and legs cutoff, knowing they would have a very uncertain and begging future seemed like cruel and unusual punishment for them.

We said goodbye to Sierra Leone for a while after seventeen years of ministry there. All CinA missionaries were evacuated and moved to other areas.

# Chapter 49

## New Ministry in Ghana, Africa

From Sierra Leone, we prayed for guidance as to where God would have us go next. Upon reading about Ghana and training a Pastor from Ghana in our London School, we were invited to run a series of crusades in Accra; Kumasi; Sunyani and Techiman

We welcomed this opportunity, and in July of 1994, we held nightly crusades for two and a half weeks, at the end of the monsoon season. Either all on our team were from Germany or the U S therefore did not know the Ghanaian weather patterns. On opening night in Kumasi at the cultural center, it rained very hard. Our program was slated for 6pm and we begin at 6:30.

The Vice President had sent word that he and a delegation of ten persons would attend the first crusade. The rains did not abate by service time, which was set at 6 pm. We waited one half hour and begin the services. At 8:30pm, we decided to close early due to the rainstorm and ferocious winds.

The next morning the assistant to the Vice President rang to state how disappointed they were that upon their arrived at 9pm, we had dismissed the service. He went on to say, that had we waited just a few more minutes, the rains would be gone and the service continued until at least 10pm.

We had not planned such long hours, however, when in Rome do as the Romans. For the remainder of the crusades, they would continue to say, "The rain will only last two hours then we will be there." Sure enough, from five to seven it would pour down then a bit past seven it would clear up. The people would then begin pouring into the meeting halls.

This new ministry is a book itself, but I won't go into all of it here. Officers were elected and the ministry was registered as a Non Government Organization (NGO) for nonprofit purposes.

For the next ten years, we planted and built twelve churches; five elementary schools; one medical clinic and one Library. We trained hundreds in our Pastor's Training Seminars. Annual Medical and Dental teams go out to assist in medical services.

Sunday school teachers, Women Ministry workers, and youth workers have all been taught to teach and build up their church ministries.

Since we have been writing this book, there seems to be times in which we have to say God brought about a pause. Again, we shall have to say that here. In the spring of 2000 upon my return from a trip to Ghana, I went for my annual physical checkup. The Doctor asked several questions and then said he had two new exams to do at this time, one for colon, and one for prostate cancer.

The old "C" word hit hard, as my mother and four siblings had died of the disease. Hoping against hope, I prayed that those tests would come back negative.

Two weeks later, our home church, Northview Community, was hosting its annual Leadership Program and I had invited Toshio Sato and four other Japanese Pastors to the event. The conference was outstanding with great motivational speakers. The men were captivated with the church growth and evangelism aspects of the teachings. After the week conference, we planned to fly to Los Angeles, rent a van, and visit two other churches that were know for their teachings on church growth.

While at Vancouver airport, I remembered that the results of my tests were to be back that same week. I rang the Doctor's office, and he came on the phone, not knowing that I was not at home." Elgin, he said, "I am afraid we have both good news and bad, the bad news is we found cancer cells in your prostate; the good news is that we found it early and it has not spread into any other areas. Come in and we can talk about farther treatment.

The next call was to Dorothy, who was just devastated and thought I should come home immediately. Well, I said it is not anything we can do right away, so I will continue the trip and return on the usual schedule.

In Los Angeles, I came down with a flu bug and was in bed in the Marriott Hotel, for the next three days, the five Japanese Pastors drove themselves to both conferences, and I could only mutter a few directions and mark the maps.

Sometimes I think God wants to show us what is most important in life. We assume that ministry and all the work for him is urgent, but he will show us differently. I was thinking how important it was to help these five pastors get around LA since I knew it so well, they had no problem at all.

I did not tell Toshio and the others about the cancer, for I was not sure what to say. I thought it best to wait and check with my Doctor before revealing such news. Returning home, I went for the appointment with fear and trembling. My family Doctor sent me to two other specialists, the oncologist, cancer specialists, who would determine the type of cancer, and the Urologists who would decide how to treat cancer in the Urinary tract.

God blessed us to have a great team of Doctors and nurses for my pending surgery. We decided that as I was in great physical shape, the surgery was best. This meant the cancer would be fully removed from the body. Other treatments are good, but the cells are still there and can reoccur at anytime.

We shall never say that this was easy it was not. God gave us many comforting scriptures assuring us that He was there. The one that flowed through my mind repeal was Psalms 23:4. NIV; "Even though I walk through the valley of the shadow of death, I will fear no evil for you are with me; your rod and your staff, they comfort me.

Family and friends wrote, rang, sent e-mails, and even visited to remind us of their prayers and best wishes. We were all claiming the promises of God for my healing and coming through this, well again. Sitting here today, I can say, "God answered that prayer!"

The surgery was April 2000 and this April 2006, the Doctor's gave me a clean cancer free signal. I will still have the annual checks to see that no other major problem develops, for I have been a type 2 diabetic for over 23years.Here again, God has blessed me to manage it through diet and now, three tablets per day. We can only say it's God who has kept us, and not we, ourselves.

It also humbled me, personally, for many of my dear friends and co-workers, with similar conditions and years younger, did not come through and are in heaven today. None of us will ever know why God takes one and leaves another, but I really felt God had more for me to do. Today I am determined to finish what he placed in my hands to do.

When people ask me about the future, I always tell them that I will be serving God for as long as he allows me good health an the ability to accomplish the task.

We are continuing the work in Ghana as our last major project. Personally, we do not desire to open more fields, but we would like to solidify and consolidate the ones that God has already given.

The work in Sierra Leone was revived after the civil war by teams from Canada led by Ken & Yvonne Wiebe. I was pleased to see the vision continued by young people, Therefore, I did not rejoin the ministry. This will allow the present team to raise funds and minister as God directs them.

We retired to Canada in 2002, however, we continue to take medical teams Sunday school training teams; Dental teams; and Pastoral training teams to assist in preparing our leaders in the ten churches.

Another unexpected development in Ghana was, that in 2001, I was crown a chief in the Kings court and my wife was crowned Queen Mother. This was an honor chosen to be bestowing upon us by Omanhene (King), Okatakyie Kudom IV. He bestowed upon me the name and title, Kwasi Kudon, Apagyahene. The name Kwasi, means born on Sunday and Apagyahene means, one who lifts the nation. I do not think I was born on Sunday, but this is a named traditionally given to Pastors, meaning Sunday man. My wife was bestowed the same title but with the female ending, Apagyahema, meaning Queen Mother who lifts the nation.

These titles only verified what we were already doing so we did not hesitate to accept the position, as it gave us the ability to speak and advise a local King. He had assured us that we would not be required to do tribal rites or oblations to the stools as non-Christians are asked to perform.

We had a vast installation service with Bishop George Thornton opening in prayer and Pastor John Jenkins reading the Scriptures. The King's Pastor prayed the prayer of commitment over us. The King then rose and touched us on the head with his sword, just as the Monarchs of Europe use in bestowing a Knighthood.

The Ohmanhene accepted Christ in 2002, and we invited him to attend our May conference as our guest. He accepted the invitation with the security stipulation that an amour-bearer (bodyguard) accompany him on the trip. During our May Missions conference, 2002, he was one of two speakers. Having lived in Britain as a Youngman, he speaks impeccable British English.

Our Sunday school children presented the King many school bags filled with school supplies for the children in his region of Brong Ahafo. . He gave a wonderful note of thanks and appreciation to the Church for funds sent to build churches, and schools as well as the water wells bored through solid rock.

**Three new supporting churches joined our team at this time. They were:**

- The Washington Christian Center pastored by Rev. McKinney, Silver Springs, MD;
- First Baptist Church Glenarden, MD, Pastored by Rev. John Jenkins;
- Galilee Baptist Church of Kent's Store, Virginia, Pastored by Rev. Otis Spellman.

**Close friends are now my right hand men and assisted me in planning the trips:**

- Leonard and Ida Johnson of Virginia,
- Paul and Gail Chatman, from First Baptist of Glenarden, MD;
- Retavis Polk and family of Tacoma, WA. a childhood friend that we have reconnected with after 35 years.

The persons listed above were the main catalysts for the launching of the Ghana expansion. Pastor Jenkins sent two missionaries to assist in the ministry, Mae Tanner and Susie Taylor; built two churches and two Parsonages and continues to send annual Vacation Bible School Teams to teach the children.

From Canada, my home church, Northview Community Church of Abbotsford, BC, set up an agreement to assist us in Ghana for five years. They planted two churches; built two parsonages; drilled seven water wells; ran annual medical and dental clinics, along with aiding our annul Pastors Training Seminars

We are ever grateful to Pastor Darcy Kuhn, John and Mary McCray, Professor and Mrs. Paul Wartman, and Dr Sam Edworthy (Dentist), and Doctors, Warren Anquist, Jim Pankrat, and Ken Dick for volunteering to go and give of themselves, that others may live. Many team members too numerous to name made the trips. Each one blessed the people of Ghana beyond measure.

Through Northview, an incredible gift from The Henry Block Foundation was donated. The foundation sent one hundred thousand dollars to translated and produce a Jesus film into a tribal language. We were also to purchase a projector; a gas generator; and screen, and support a film team for four years.

This was a fantastic blessing and provided a marvelous tool of evangelism for Ghana. It also brought back memories of the way our village ministry had begun in Japan almost 50 years ago! We were able to give instructions from experience for the seating and set up, as well as how to keep the meeting short.

At first, our team gave long sermons, but we reminded that they are speaking to the unconverted, which would soon walk out if they made the sermon long or had long closings. Gradually, they are showing growth through practice. They are able to reduce the showing times to 90 minutes instead of 120 minutes.

At this writing, we have a team of pastors and leaders in place to keep the ministry moving smoothly. They are President, Pastor Jacob Nangai; Secretary, Patrick Yaw; Treasurer, Pastor Samuel Bediako; and member, Pastor James Hayford.

We will conclude here by stating, that a new and exhilarating door of ministry has opened for us at this stage in life and we endeavor to write more about it later. Thank you for investing in our ministry!

We appreciate each and everyone who has assisted us though the years, without you none of this would have been possible and without Christ, our savior and Lord, nothing would have been accomplished! To God Be the Glory.

Ghana Medical Missions

Team from North view Church, Canada

Medical Exam

Dental Exam

# 2005 Northview Team

## School Buildings and Youth Outreach

Ghana Schools are still open to the Gospel

Building a school costs, $ 10,000

There are 3 to 4 students to each desk.

Church Planting

Pastor Darcy
Kuhn Prays
Prayer of
Dedication

The
Nkoranza
Church

Dedication
Service
2004

Maryland Outreach Teams

First Baptist Church of
Glenarden, MD sends
annual ministry teams.

## First Baptist Sends Out
## Two Fulltime Missionaries

The First Baptist of GA, Maryland trained
and sent out two fulltime Missionaries,
shown above, Susie Taylor and Mae Tanner

Team
Leader
Sylvia Taylor
Shares at a
local church

Water Wells Bored down through
Granite Rock over 249 ft

# Women's Ministry

Crowned A Chief
in 2001

King presenting the new
Apagyahene and Apagyahema

# Village Outreach

Ayerede Church Dedication
by Pastor John Jenkins of Maryland.

# 2005 Northview Team

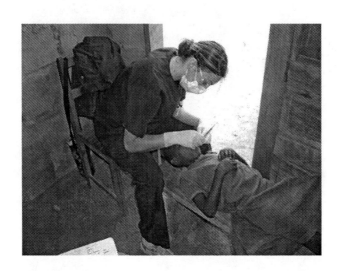

Our Ghana Team 2006

Dorothy, Elgin, Lenwood, Yvonne,
Linda and Retavis.

Lenwood Johnson greets the local
Chiefs.

# Ghana Ministry

Elgin & Pastor Justin Praying for the King

Our 3 sons, Willis, Timothy, and Michael ministering with us in Ghana, 2003

Son, Willis, held four youth concerts 2005

Taylor Family 2006, minus one grandson, Vierra, 21.

Dorothy, Willis, Timothy, Michael, & Elgin

Remaining Fruit

Brenda
was led to
Christ by
Bro. Elgin
in 1976.

Pastor & Mrs. Ron
Hammond of Golden
Triangle, Church on
the Rock,
Beaumont, Texas

Printed in the United States
93220LV00003B/301-354/A